Everyday English Handbook for International Learners

Bruce Wm. Franz

Copyright© 2018 Bruce Wm. Franz

ISBN: 978-1-62249-447-7

Published by
Biblio Publishing
BiblioPublishing.com
Columbus, Ohio

Table of Contents

Part I	1
Vocabulary and Sample Sentences	
a	3
Grammar Break: Verb Tenses	11
b	16
c	21
Grammar Break: Articles	30
d	32
e	38
f	44
g	51
Grammar Break: Basic Comma Rules	53
h	56
i	60
j	65
k	66
l	67
Grammar Break: Using Either and Neither	70
m	72
n	77
o	81
p	85
Grammar Break: Past Tense Sounds	92
q	94
r	95
s	101
Grammar Break: Using Should, Could, and Would	114
t	116
Grammar Break: Irregular Verbs	121
v	123
w	125
y	128
z	130
Part II: Idioms, Slang, Expressions	131
a	133
b	134
c	136
d	139
e	140
f	141
g	142
h	145
i	149
j	151
k	151
l	153
m	154
n	155
o	156
p	158
r	159
Grammar Break: Phrasal Verbs	161
s	162
t	164
u	166
w	166
y	168

FOREWORD

This book is written for ESOL (English for Speakers of Foreign Languages) learners who want to improve their English language skills. Included in this book are common vocabulary words and expressions that you might encounter anywhere in the United States. We call these common expressions IDIOMS. These are expressions that cannot be understood from meanings of the separate words in the expressions. The expression or idiom has its own different meaning. Idioms are common in English, and using them will help your English sound more natural. It will help your English conversation by learning to use some of these idioms.

New vocabulary is a large part of improving your communication. The vocabulary presented here is common in American speech and writing. The vocabulary is presented in a way that will help you learn, understand, and remember the words. Bits of grammar and tips to help you are scattered throughout the book. You will find such things as **VERB TENSES, COMMA RULES, IRREGULAR VERBS,** and more within these pages. We hope all of this will make you a better English speaker!

v

PART I

VOCABULARY and SAMPLE SENTENCES

a.

TO ABANDON = to leave and never return to someone or something, or to leave a place because of danger.

Her husband ABANDONED her and the children."
"Some people ABANDON their old cars."
"The forest fire caused many people to ABANDON their homes."
"People who have unwanted cats or dogs sometimes take them out to the country and ABANDON them."

TO ABDUCT = to take someone away by force

"Don't let anyone ABDUCT your baby while you are shopping."
"Have you heard stories of people claiming to be ABDUCTED by aliens?"
"In 1932, a famous case was when the 20-month-old baby of Charles Lindbergh was ABDUCTED from his home in New Jersey and killed. A man was arrested and found guilty, and he was executed."

ABRUPT = very sudden and not expected; talking to others in a short, unfriendly way

"I had to make an ABRUPT stop when a child ran into the street."
"Be friendly when you speak with others. Don't be ABRUPT."
"I asked him a question, and his answer was an ABRUPT "No."

ABSENT = not present

"My son was sick and ABSENT from school yesterday."
"The employees were ready for the meeting, but the company President was ABSENT."
"We have 24 students here today, but we should have 25. Who is ABSENT?"

TO ACCOMPANY = to go together with someone; to be included with something

"I like my wife to ACCOMPANY me to the doctor's office. It helps to have two people hear and remember what the doctor says."
"Vegetables ACCOMPANIED the meal I ordered."

ACCUSTOMED = familiar with something so that it seems normal

"I am not yet ACCUSTOMED to living in Columbus."
"Are you ACCUSTOMED to getting up early every day?"
"Don't get ACCUSTOMED to sitting around this summer. Get out and get a job!"

ACCURATE = correct; with no mistakes

"Is this number ACCURATE?"
"My address is not ACCURATE. I have moved."
"She gave us an ACCURATE description of the man who stole her purse."

TO ACQUIRE = to get or obtain

"Where can I ACQUIRE a passport?"
"He ACQUIRED a lot of money when he sold his business."
"She ACQUIRED a ready-made family when she married a man who had two children."

ADDRESS = the number on a house or building

"The ADDRESS of my house is 115 South Main Street."
"When you move, give the post office a change of ADDRESS card."
"I looked up Steve's ADDRESS on the computer."

TO ADDRESS = to speak to a person or group

"The President will ADDRESS the nation tonight. "
"Abraham Lincoln gave his famous Gettysburg ADDRESS in November, 1863."

ADEQUATE = enough for some requirement; acceptable

"There has not been ADEQUATE rain for my garden."
"Will this room be ADEQUATE for you?"
"Our restaurant meal was nothing special, but it was ADEQUATE."

ADJACENT = next to or beside

"My house is ADJACENT to the park."
"Our ADJACENT neighbor works for the school."
"The new school will be built ADJACENT to the post office."

TO ADJUST = to change the position of something

"Your tie is not straight. Let me ADJUST it for you."
"He ADJUSTED his glasses before he began to speak."
"It's too cold in here. ADJUST the thermostat a little higher."

TO ADMIRE = to feel approval for someone or something; to look at something with enjoyment

"I ADMIRE the President for the work he is doing."

"We ADMIRE the beautiful scenery."
"They ADMIRED the house, but it was too expensive."

AFFABLE = friendly; easy to talk to

"Your uncle is a very AFFABLE fellow."
"We had an AFFABLE conversation."
"The salesman wasn't very AFFABLE with us. We should go somewhere else."

ALIBI = an excuse for not being somewhere or doing something

"Where were you when the bank was robbed? What is your ALIBI?"
"I wasn't there when it happened. I was at school. That's my ALIBI."
"He didn't have an ALIBI, so the police arrested him."

TO ALLUDE = to speak of or mention something indirectly

"Tell me more about what you ALLUDED to a few minutes ago."
"He ALLUDED that he might move to Chicago."
"Please don't ALLUDE to our conversation. I don't want anyone to know that we talked."

AMENABLE = agreeable; willing to accept something

"I don't want to cook. Are you AMENABLE to going out for dinner?"
"I try to be AMENABLE most of the time."
"They were not AMENABLE to my suggestion."

AMENITIES = things that make life easier or more pleasant

"Our hotel had many AMENITIES: pool, restaurant, free cable TV."
"Electricity, hot water, and indoor plumbing are AMENITIES I enjoy that my grandfather didn't have."
"I'd like to accept your job offer, but first tell me about the AMENITIES."

TO AMPUTATE = to cut off part of a person's body

"He was in a terrible accident and the doctors had to AMPUTATE his leg."
"The decision to AMPUTATE was not easy."

TO ANALYZE = to study and examine something closely

"Let's ANALYZE the problem and find a solution."
"The water must be ANALYZED before it is approved for drinking."
"Let's ANALYZE the situation before we agree."

ANCESTOR = a person from someone's family in the past

"My ANCESTORS came to the US from Germany in 1853."
"Many people like to track their ANCESTORS through genealogy."
"I researched my genealogy and found one of my mother's ANCESTORS in England in 1620."

ANGEL = 1. A spiritual being from Heaven

"An ANGEL appeared to Mary and said she would have a baby to be named Jesus."

ANGEL = 2. a good, kind person

"Your son is an ANGEL."
"Be an ANGEL and get me a cup of coffee."
"A very thin pasta is called ANGEL hair pasta."

ANGLE = the intersection where two lines meet

"A triangle has three ANGLES."
"The road makes a sharp ANGLE by my house."
"That man has an ANGLED forehead."

ANNUAL = happening once a year

"The company has an ANNUAL Christmas party in December."
"I have to see my doctor for an ANNUAL checkup."

ANONYMOUS = not named or identified

"We don't know who wrote it. The author is ANONYMOUS."
"The gift is from an ANONYMOUS donor."
"The police received an ANONYMOUS tip about the robbery."

TO ASSERT = to say something in a strong, definite way

"He ASSERTS that he will never do it again."
"Despite the evidence, he ASSERTS that he is innocent."

TO ASTOUND = to surprise greatly

"The magician will ASTOUND you with his tricks."
"I've seen everything. Nothing ASTOUNDS me."
"I'm ASTOUNDED to see you! You said you would be gone three months! What happened?"

ATROCIOUS = Very bad, or very cruel

"Doctors often have ATROCIOUS handwriting."
"It's ATROCIOUS the way he treats his wife and children."
"The food was ATROCIOUS! I'll never go back there again!"

ATTIRE = clothing

"Proper ATTIRE is required at the restaurant."
"Formal ATTIRE is to be worn for the party."
"I want to wear my best ATTIRE for dinner with the President."
"The stores will begin to display their Halloween ATTIRE in September."

AUCTION = a public sale where things are sold to the highest bidder

"I bought a table at the AUCTION."
"Some people like to go to AUCTIONS just to watch the sale."
"We could sell our furniture at a garage sale, or we could have an AUCTION."

AUDACITY = a personal quality that is seen as shocking or rude

"He had the AUDACITY to say that the divorce was all my fault!"
"It takes AUDACITY to tell the boss that his idea is no good."
"She doesn't have the AUDACITY to ask for a raise."

AUTHORITY = the power to make decisions and give orders

"The boss has the AUTHORITY to approve vacation time."
"My wife and I share the AUTHORITY in our house."
"Who is in AUTHORITY here?"

AVERSE = strongly opposed to something

"I am AVERSE to same sex marriages."
"We are AVERSE to people smoking in our house."
"We've already moved once. I'm AVERSE to moving again."

AWARE = knowing that a problem or situation exists

"Are you AWARE of any problems?"
"I'm sorry to wake you. I was not AWARE you were asleep."
"I would have stopped at the grocery store, but I wasn't AWARE that we needed anything."

AWKWARD = not graceful, or not easy to deal with

"His ex-wife was at the meeting. It was an AWKWARD situation."
"He is an AWKWARD dancer"

GRAMMAR BREAK: VERB TENSES

SIMPLE PRESENT
I cook dinner every day

SIMPLE PAST
I cooked dinner yesterday

SIMPLE FUTURE
I will cook dinner tomorrow

PRESENT CONTINUOUS
i am cooking dinner now

PAST CONTINUOUS
I was cooking dinner yesterday

FUTURE CONTINUOUS
I will be cooking dinner tomorrow

PRESENT PERFECT
I have cooked dinner many times

PAST PERFECT
I had cooked dinner when he got home

FUTURE PERFECT
I will have cooked dinner every day this week

PRESENT PERFECT CONTINUOUS
I have been cooking dinner all day

PAST PERFECT CONTINUOUS
I had been cooking when he called

FUTURE PERFECT CONTINUOUS
By the end of the day, I will have been cooking for 12 hours.

The VERB TENSES

The verb tense names are not very important in conversational English. What is important is knowing when and how to use them! Most Americans can't tell you what tense they are using, but they do use them properly...usually! Pay attention below how the tenses are formed and how they are used in sentences.

The **SIMPLE PRESENT TENSE** has two main uses: for action happening right now, or when it happens regularly. Most regular verbs use the basic form.

first person singular: I work
first person plural: We work
second person singular: You work
second person plural: You work
third person singular: He or she works
(note the "s")
third person plural: They work

The **PRESENT PERFECT TENSE** refers to an action that occurs at an indefinite time in the past or has begun in the past and continues to the present time. We form the PRESENT PERFECT TENSE by using HAVE or HAS with the past participle.

"He HAS BROKEN his leg."
"We HAVE EATEN our dinner."
"They HAVE BEEN calling you."
"She HAS SEEN that movie."

The **PRESENT CONTINUOUS TENSE** indicates that an action or condition is happening now, or frequently, and may continue in the future. We form the PRESENT CONTINUOUS TENSE by using AM, IS, or ARE with the present participle (the verb ending with "-ing").

"He IS TALKING to his brother."
"She IS WASHING her hair."
"We ARE COMING to see you." "They ARE HAVING a party."

The **PRESENT PERFECT CONTINUOUS TENSE** refers to an unspecified time before now, and may still be going on, or may have just finished. We form the PRESENT PERFECT CONTINUOUS TENSE by using HAVE BEEN or HAS BEEN with the present participle (verb ending with "-ing.")

"I HAVE BEEN WAITING for you."
"We HAVE BEEN PLAYING with the children."
"She HAS BEEN COOKING all day."
"They HAVE BEEN SHOPPING at the mall."

The **SIMPLE PAST TENSE** is used to talk about things that happened before this moment, something that has already happened. For regular verbs, we add "-ed" or "-d" if the verb ends in "e."

"I CALLED him last night."
"She TIED her shoes."
"We WALKED to the theater."
"He CARRIED the baby to bed."

The **PAST PERFECT TENSE** talks about something that happened before something else in the past. We form the PAST PERFECT TENSE by using HAD with the past participle.

"I HAD BEEN to the bank when my wife called my cell phone."
"She HAD CHANGED the channel when I came back in the room."
"You HAD TALKED to him before I saw him."
"They HAD DRIVEN a few miles when the engine stopped."

The **PAST CONTINUOUS TENSE** describes actions or events before now that are still going on at the time of speaking. It expresses an unfinished action in the past. We form the PAST CONTINUOUS

TENSE by using WAS or WERE with the present participle (verb ending in "-ing").

"She WAS WATCHING TV when the phone rang."
"We WERE COMING home when we saw him."
"When we arrived he WAS TAKING a shower.
"The police knocked on the door when I WAS EATING my dinner."

The **PAST PERFECT CONTINUOUS TENSE** shows that an action that started in the past continued until another time in the past. We form the PAST PERFECT CONTINUOUS TENSE by using HAD BEEN with the present participle (the verb ending in "-ing").

"I HAD BEEN EXERCISING when I felt sick."
"They HAD BEEN CLEANING the house when they smelled smoke."
"We HAD BEEN FREEZING because the window was open."
"He HAD BEEN SMOKING before we knew it."

The **SIMPLE FUTURE TENSE** talks about an action or condition that will begin and end in the future. We form the SIMPLE FUTURE TENSE by using WILL with the basic verb.

"He WILL LEAVE in the morning."
"She WILL BE in class on Friday."
"I WILL WORK at home tomorrow."
"They WILL DRIVE to Florida."

The **FUTURE PERFECT TENSE** is used for actions that will be completed before some other future point. We form the FUTURE PERFECT TENSE by using WILL HAVE with the past participle.

"They WILL HAVE BEEN here three hours at 6:00 PM."
"She WILL HAVE MARRIED me before her family knows it."

"We WILL HAVE TOLD him before they can tell him."
"I WILL HAVE CLEANED it before they can see it."

The **FUTURE CONTINUOUS TENSE** indicates that something will occur in the future and continue for an unspecified length of time . We form the FUTURE CONTINUOUS TENSE by using WILL BE with the present participle (the verb with "-ing").

"We WILL BE BABYSITTING our grandchildren tomorrow."
"She WILL BE FIXING dinner for all of us."
"They WILL BE MOVING to Florida ."
"I WILL BE WRITING a book for ESL students."

The **FUTURE PERFECT CONTINUOUS TENSE** describes action that will continue up to a point in the future. We form the FUTURE PERFECT CONTINUOUS TENSE by using WILL HAVE BEEN with the present participle (the verb with "-ing").

"This summer, we WILL HAVE BEEN COMING to Cleveland for six years."
"On Friday, they WILL HAVE BEEN VISITING us for two weeks. When are they going home?"
"We WILL HAVE BEEN FISHING for two hours. Do you think we will catch any fish?"

b.

BANKRUPT = unable to pay bills

"After several years of business, the company went BANKRUPT."
"If we cannot control our spending, we will be BANKRUPT."

BANQUET = a formal dinner for many people, especially to celebrate a special event

"The company is planning a BANQUET for all the new employees."
"They held a special BANQUET to celebrate his retirement."
"The wedding BANQUET will be held downstairs at the church after the ceremony."

" TO BELITTLE = to describe something or someone as unimportant

"I was very embarrassed when the teacher BELITTLED me in front of the class."
"The book critic BELITTLED the author's work."
"It's not nice to BELITTLE someone."

BELLIGERENT = angry and aggressive

"The woman became BELLIGERENT when they refused to help her."
"Some people drink too much and start acting BELLIGERENT."
"The two countries are being BELLIGERENT. I hope it doesn't lead to war."

TO BEHOOVE = to be advisable to do something for one's own good or for others

"It will BEHOOVE you to work hard if you want to advance in this company."
"It BEHOOVES us all to remember to vote."
"I think you can find a better job. It would BEHOOVE you to try a little harder."

BENEVOLENT = kind and generous

"They made a BENEVOLENT donation to the charity."
"My uncle was a BENEVOLENT man."
"Some churches have a BENEVOLENT fund to help people in need."

BENIGN = 1. not cancerous

"He was relieved that his tumor was BENIGN."

BENIGN = 2. not causing harm or damage

"The chemical is BENIGN to the environment."

BEWILDERED = very much confused

"I am BEWILDERED by all the traffic in and around the city."
"She had a BEWILDERED look on her face."
"We were BEWILDERED when they told us they didn't want us as tutors any more."

BIDDY = an old woman, especially one who is annoying

"The woman next door is a nosy, old BIDDY."
"The old BIDDY should mind her own business."
"The BIDDIES like to get together and gossip about all the neighbors."

BIGOTED = having or showing a strong, unfair dislike of other people or ideas

"He has always been BIGOTED towards women."
"Many people were offended by his BIGOTED statements."
"President Trump seems to be BIGOTED against countries in Africa."

TO BLAME = to say or think that someone is responsible for something bad that has happened

"Don't BLAME me! I didn't do it!"
"The company BLAMES the poor economy for its slow sales."
"Was anyone to BLAME for the accident?"

TO BLINDSIDE = 1. To hit someone who is driving or facing another direction
2. to surprise of shock someone unpleasantly

"His car ran the stop sign and BLINDSIDED my car."
"We were BLINDSIDED by the news of his death."
"It was completely unexpected. The decision BLINDSIDED us."

TO BLUSH = to become red in your face when you are embarrassed or ashamed

"I BLUSHED when the class told me I forgot to zip my pants."
"She BLUSHED with embarrassment when they complimented her."
"The student BLUSHED when the teacher caught him sleeping in class."

"TO BOLSTER = to make something or someone be better or stronger; to give support to someone

"My wife came with me to BOLSTER my confidence."
"The good news BOLSTERED his spirits."

"He's been unhappy lately. What can we do to BOLSTER his attitude?"

BOONDOGGLE = a useless trip; work or activity that is wasteful or pointless

"His trip to California was a BOONDOGGLE. They didn't accomplish anything."
"The new road is a BOONDOGGLE: over budget, behind schedule, and unnecessary."
"The trip to the store was a BOONDOGGLE. They didn't have what I wanted."

TO BOOST = 1. to increase the power or amount of something
2. a push upwards

"The company want to BOOST its sales."
"She takes vitamins to BOOST her energy."
"He BOOSTED me up, and I climbed over the wall."

BRIEF = lasting a short period of time, or using only a few words

"She worked there a BRIEF three weeks."
"He gave a BRIEF description of his plan."
"It should be a BRIEF meeting. I think I'll be home soon."

TO BRIEF = to give information or instruction to someone

"The manager BRIEFED us about the new procedures."
"I have to BRIEF the boss this morning."
"Keep me BRIEFED on the progress of the job."

BUDGET (noun) = an amount of money available for spending

"We are on a BUDGET to spend less money,"
"Our monthly BUDGET for food is $400."
"The US BUDGET is millions of dollars."

TO BUDGET = to make a plan for spending money, or to plan your time

"If we BUDGET carefully, we can take a vacation this fall."
"We have a lot to do today. Let's BUDGET our time and get everything finished."
"They didn't BUDGET for our project. We'll have to wait until next year."

BULKY = 1. Large and difficult to carry or store 2. a large and fat or muscular person

"This box is BULKY. Help me carry it upstairs."
"American football players are often big and BULKY."
"The chairs are too BULKY to put in the car. We need a truck."

BYE BYE is an informal way to say, "Goodbye."

"On the telephone, I might say, 'BYE BYE!' Talk to you later!"
"In person, I might say, 'BYE BYE!' See you tomorrow!"
"BYE BYE, everyone! Have a good weekend! I'll see you next week!"

C.

TO CANCEL = to stop doing or planning to do something

"We had to CANCEL our dinner reservation."
"I CANCELED my dentist appointment."
"The customer called to CANCEL her order."

CAPABLE = able to do something or skilled at doing something

"Many cell phones are CAPABLE of connecting to the Internet."
"She is a very CAPABLE student."
"I don't think he's CABABLE to do the job. We should hire someone else."

CATASTROPHE = a terrible disaster

"The airplane crash was a CATASTROPHE. All the people were killed."
"The forest fires and mudslides were a CATASTROPHE in California."
"This job is a CATASTROPHE. Take it apart and start over."

TO CHAR = to cook or burn something until it was black

"Please watch the oven and don't let the potatoes CHAR."
"He CHARRED the hamburgers on the grill."
"The fire next door CHARRED the side of my house."

CHEAPSKATE = someone who doesn't like to spend money

"His daughter married a CHEAPSKATE."
"Don't be such a CHEAPSKATE. You can afford to take your wife out to dinner."
"He's such a CHEAPSKATE that he probably still has the first dollar he ever earned."

CHEERFUL = feeling or showing happiness

"He always seems to be CHEERFUL." "She's a very CHEERFUL person."
"It was a CHEERFUL party. Everyone had a good time."

CHRONIC = 1. Continuing for a long time 2. always or often doing something

"Smoking has given him a CHRONIC cough."
"Crime in big cities is a CHRONIC problem."
"He is a CHRONIC alcoholic. He won't join Alcoholics Anonymous."

CIVILIAN = not military or police or firefighter

"I was a CIVILIAN employee at Wright-Patterson Air Force Base."
"The police ordered the CIVILIANS to stand back."
"The military hospital cannot accept CIVILIAN patients."

TO CLAP = to applaud; to hit the hands of your palms together to show approval

"The children all CLAPPED their hands."
"The people stood and CLAPPED after the performance."
"Let's all stand and CLAP when he comes into the room."

CLEAVAGE = the space between a woman's breasts, especially when it can be seen

"Her low-cut dress showed a lot of CLEAVAGE."
"The photographer's pictures had too much CLEAVAGE for the newspaper to use."

CLOUT = the power to control or influence situations

"Do you have the CLOUT to get me a job where you work?"
"I don't have any CLOUT around here."
"It took a lot of CLOUT to make them agree."

COARSE = 1. having a rough quality
2. rude or offensive

"People used to tell me that I have COARSE hair."
"He uses a lot of COARSE language."
"I need some COARSE sandpaper, not the fine sandpaper."

TO COINCIDE = 1. to happen at the same time as something else
2. to be in agreement

"My birthday COINCIDES with Thanksgiving this year."
"If our schedules COINCIDE, we can ride together."
"His plans don't COINCIDE with mine."

COINCIDENCE = a situation in which events happen at the same time in a way that is not expected or planned

"I met an old classmate at the bank today. It was a COINCIDENCE that we were both there at the same time."
"What a COINCIDENCE! I never expected to see you here!"
"I thought my wallet was lost. It was a lucky COINCIDENCE that someone found and returned it. I was happy to give him a reward."

COLLEAGUE = a person who works with you

"I heard from one of my old COLLEAGUES. He lives in Las Vegas now."
"Sometimes he has lunch with some of his COLLEAGUES."
"I'd like to introduce you to my COLLEAGUES."

COHERENT = 1. easy to understand
2. able to talk clearly

"Someone called for you but he wasn't COHERENT. I don't know who it was or what he wanted."
"He has a COHERENT plan to address our financial problems."
"She made a COHERENT argument for her client."

TO COMPEL = to force someone to do something

"I'd like you to come with me, but if you're busy, I won't COMPEL you."
"He didn't have a car. I was COMPELLED to take him to work."
"You can't COMPEL me to do it."

TO COMPREHEND = TO UNDERSTAND [*often used in negative statements*]

"I cannot COMPREHEND how they could treat their children so badly."
"We don't COMPREHEND much about the new technology."
"Did you COMPREHEND his explanation?"

TO COMMISERATE = to express sadness or sympathy for someone who has experienced something unpleasant

"The team members COMMISERATED over the loss of the game."
"I can COMMISERATE with him. The same thing happened to me."

"You cannot COMMISERATE how much I have lost."

TO CONCEAL = to hide something, or to keep something secret

"He had a gun CONCEALED under his coat."
"She tried to CONCEAL her disappointment."
"He CONCEALED the stolen money, and it was never found."

CONCEPT = an idea about something or how it works

"Computer companies are always exploring new CONCEPTS."
"I have no CONCEPT of how it works."
"Please explain your CONCEPT to us."

CONCERNED = feeling worry, or caring about something

"He doesn't look well. I'm CONCERNED about his health."
"She's CONCERNED because her husband hasn't called her."
"I'm CONCERNED that we won't have enough money."

TO CONFER = to talk about or discuss something

"We want to CONFER with our son's teacher about his behavior."
"The doctors CONFERRED to decide the best treatment for the patient."
"Did you CONFER with her? What did she say?"

TO CONFIDE = to tell someone a secret or private matter while trusting them not to repeat it

"He CONFIDED to his friends that he and his wife were getting a divorce."
"If I CONFIDE in you, I don't want you to tell anyone else."
"We can't CONFIDE in anyone. We don't want anyone to know

what we did."

CONSCIOUS = 1. awake and able to understand what is going on around you
2. to be aware of something

"The patient was CONSCIOUS during his surgery."
"Are you CONSCIOUS of how late it is?"
"I'm not CONSCIOUS of any problems he was having."

CONFIDENT = 1. have a feeling that you can do something well
2. certain that something is true or will happen

"I am CONFIDENT I can do a good job for you."
"They are CONFIDENT that the economy will improve."

CONFRONTATION = a situation in which people in groups fight or oppose each other in an angry way

"The Democrats and Republicans are having CONFRONTATIONS over taxes and immigration."
"I had a CONFRONTATION with my neighbor about his dog digging in my yard."
"Calm down. Don't let your argument become a CONFRONTATION."

"TO CONSTRUCT = to build or make something

"They plan to CONSTRUCT a new hospital on the west side of town."
"Several new houses will be CONSTRUCTED this year."
"He CONSTRUCTED a careful argument for his plans."

TO CONSUME = to eat something, or to use

something such as time, fuel, or resources

"We CONSUMED all the food they brought us.
"Too much of his time is CONSUMED on the computer."
"We can't CONSUME all of this. Let's put some of it in the freezer."

**CONTAGIOUS = 1. having a sickness that can be passed to someone else
2. causing other people to feel or act in a similar way**

"My cold may be CONTAGIOUS. Stay back and don't come close to me."
"He has a CONTAGIOUS laugh. If you hear him, you will laugh, too!"
"The hospital keeps CONTAGIOUS patients in a special area."

TO CONTEMPLATE = to think deeply and carefully about something

"We're CONTEMPLATING a move to Chicago."
"The doctor asked him if he had ever CONTEMPLATED hurting himself."
"I cannot CONTEMPLATE why he did that."

TO CONTEND = to argue or state something in a strong, definite way

"I CONTEND that same sex marriage is a sin."
"The government CONTENDS that the new tax laws will benefit everyone."
"The prisoner CONTENDS that he didn't kill the man."

CONTROVERSY = a public and often heated disagreement

"There's a lot of CONTROVERSY about allowing abortions."
"President Trump's comments raise a lot of CONTROVERSY."

"What's the CONTROVERSY here? Why are you arguing?"

CORDIAL = warm and friendly

"We had a very CORDIAL meeting."
"Everyone was quite CORDIAL."
"The salesman wasn't very CORDIAL with us."

CORPSE = a dead body

"They found a CORPSE floating in the river."
"He wanted his CORPSE to be donated to the medical school."
"The firemen found a CORPSE in the burned building."

COURTEOUS = very polite

"It was COURTEOUS of him to help carry my packages."
"She is always very COURTEOUS."
"That wasn't very COURTEOUS. Apologize to the woman."

CREDIBLE = able to be believed

"He gave a CREDIBLE excuse for being late."
"I have CREDIBLE information that the company is going to move."
"The witness was not CREDIBLE. He could not have seen the accident."

CRISIS = a difficult or dangerous situation that needs attention

"The hurricane in Puerto Rico is a CRISIS for the people."
"She has a family CRISIS and won't be in to work today."
"What might we have done to avoid the CRISIS?"

TO CRITIQUE = to give your opinion about the good and bad parts of something *[such as a piece of writing, a*

performance, or a piece of art]

"I've written an essay for school. Would you CRITIQUE it before I take it to class?"
"They met to CRITIQUE the artist's paintings."
"She gave it a very bad CRITIQUE. I have to make a lot of changes to it."

CRUCIAL = very important

"It's CRUCIAL that you be home by 4:00 PM. I must have the car then."
"We had a CRUCIAL meeting to decide what to do next."
"It's CRUCIAL that we get him to the hospital right away."

CURFEW = an order or law that requires people to be indoors after a certain time of night

"The city has a 10:00 PM CURFEW for children to be off the streets."
"I gave my daughter a 12:00 PM CURFEW to be home."
"If I'm not home by CURFEW, my Dad will be angry."

CURVACEOUS = (of a woman) having a shapely, attractively curved body

"All the models were CURVACEOUS."
"Marilyn Monroe was a CURVACEOUS actress."
"He took pictures of all the CURVACEOUS women on the beach."

> **GRAMMAR BREAK: ARTICLES**
>
> A, AN, and THE are called ARTICLES in English grammar. These are sometimes difficult for English learners. Do you use articles in your native language? They are important in spoken and written English, so here are some tips for you.

A and **AN** are used before general nouns, not specific ones. **A** is used before singular nouns that begin with a consonant.
A baby: "My daughter is going to have A baby!"
A car: "We have to buy A new car."
A desk: "Is there A desk in your room?"
A job: "Quit sitting and go get A job."
A tomato: "I'd like A tomato on my sandwich."

AN is used before singular nouns that begin with a vowel.
AN apple: "Would you like AN apple?"
AN egg: "No, I want AN egg."
AN ice cream cone: "How about AN ice cream cone?"
AN onion: "That's better than AN onion."
AN umbrella: "Bring AN umbrella. It might rain."

THE is used before singular or plural nouns to indicate the specific or certain one ones.
THE book: "Bring me THE book that's on my desk."
THE chairs: "Put THE chairs around the table."
THE dog: "THE dog has fleas."
THE men: "THE men go to work at 7:00 AM."
THE tree: "THE tree will lose its leaves in the fall."

We do not use an article with **uncountable words** (water, advice).
"Do you want water?"
"Give me your advice."

Often we use **A** to mention something the first time, then change to **THE** to be more specific.
"I was talking to **a** boy. **The** boy was crying."

We use **THE** when it is obvious what we are talking about.
"Please shut **THE** door."
"I read **THE** newspaper."
"What's **THE** date today?

We DON'T use **A** or **AN** before meals.
"I had lunch at work."

We DON'T use **A** or **AN** with school or college when we are talking about them.
"My son isn't in school yet."
"His daughter goes to college."

We use **THE** before the names of shops or where we go for service.
"I need to stop at **THE** bank."
"What do you want from **THE** grocery store?
"My car is at **THE** repair shop."
"I have to go to **THE** doctor.."

d.

TO DAWDLE = to move or act slowly

"Take a 10-minute break, but please don't DAWDLE. Be back on time."

"We don't have to be back yet. Let's DAWDLE a few more minutes."

"They DAWDLED through the mall most of the afternoon."

DEADBEAT = a person who does not pay money that is owed

"Don't loan him any money. He's a DEADBEAT, and he won't pay you back."

"Men who won't pay their ex-wives to support their children are called DEADBEAT DADS."

"We all went out for lunch, but one DEADBEAT said he didn't have any money."

DEADLINE = a date or time that something must be finished, or the last day or time that something will be accepted

"The DEADLINE for all reports is 4:00 PM tomorrow. Don't be late!"

"Tuesday is the DEADLINE to register for class."

"Are you going to meet the DEADLINE for this job?"

DEADLOCKED = unable to make an agreement or decision

"The Democrats and Republicans are DEADLOCKED. Neither side will agree."
"The jury was DEADLOCKED. Half said guilty, and half said innocent."
"If the company doesn't break the DEADLOCK, the men will go on strike."

DEBATE = A discussion between people in which they present different opinions about something [furthermore, a DEBATE may be an organized event, an informal discussion between two people, or a general discussion involving several people]

"My wife and I have a DEBATE whether to go to Cleveland on Wednesday or Thursday."
"The high school DEBATE team will meet at 2:00 PM today."

DEBT = money or something that is owed

"Some people carry a lot of DEBT on their credit cards."
"I owe you a DEBT of gratitude for helping me."
"I don't like to be in DEBT. I pay my bills as soon as I can."

TO DECLINE = 1. to say no to something
2. to become worse
3. to become less in amount or number

"I made him an offer, but he DECLINED it."
"His health has been DECLINING for several months.
"Our sales have DECLINED this month."

TO DEMOLISH = to destroy; to tear down

"The car was DEMOLISHED in the accident."

"The city is going to DEMOLISH the old school."
"Our basket ball team won the game, 98 to 37. We DEMOLISHED the other team!"

DEPRESSED = 1. feeling sad
2. having little economic activity and few jobs

"Some people feel DEPRESSED in the wintertime."
"This is a DEPRESSED area since the factory closed."
"If you are DEPRESSED, maybe you should see a doctor."

DERMATOLOGIST = a doctor who specializes in the treatment of skin problems

"She has an appointment with the DERMATOLOGIST this afternoon."
"The DERMATOLOGIST said the baby's rash is nothing to worry about."
"Our daughter is in medical school to become a DERMATOLOGIST."

DESERT = an area of dry land usually covered with sand and very hot

"The Gobi Desert is in China, and the Sahara Desert is in Africa."
"Many settlers lost their lives trying to cross the desert."
"It's hard to find any water in the DESERT."

DESPITE = without being prevented by something

"DESPITE the rain, we kept driving."
"The doctors did the surgery DESPITE his objections."
"DESPITE everything he tried, he couldn't find an answer."

DESSERT = a sweet food eaten after the main part of the meal

"I baked an apple pie for DESSERT."
"Would you like a cup of coffee with your DESSERT?"

"We had a nice meal at the restaurant, but we skipped DESSERT."

TO DETEST = to dislike something very strongly

"I DETEST all the traffic in and around the city."
"She DETESTS working with him."
"I DETEST telling her, but someone has to do it."

TO DEVOUR = to eat all of something, or to eat very quickly

"He DEVOURED everything on his plate."
"Slow down! Don't DEVOUR your food!"
"I threw out some breadcrumbs for the birds, and they DEVOURED them."

DILEMMA = a difficult decision

"It's a DILEMMA. I haven't decided what to do."
"He's faced with a DILEMMA. Should he do it or not?"
"I don't see the DILEMMA. It's either YES or NO."

TO DISCARD = to throw something away

"Read this, then DISCARD it."
"Do you want to keep this, or shall I DISCARD it?"
"These are important papers. Please don't DISCARD them."

DISTRAUGHT = very upset, so much so that you can't think clearly or behave normally

"The family was DISTRAUGHT while waiting for news of the accident."
"She was so DUSTRAUGHT that we couldn't comfort her."
"Try not to get DISTRAUGHT. I'll take care of it."

DOGGONE = an exclamation of exasperation or anger [more polite than saying DAMN]

"DOGGONE it, we're late again. Please hurry up!"
"DOGGONE, where did I leave my keys?"
"Just a DOGGONE minute! Give me a chance to explain!"

DREARY = causing unhappiness or sadness

"It's a cold, gray, DREARY day."
"He had a DREARY look on his face."
"I'm getting tired of winter. I don't want to hear another DREARY weather report."

TO DRENCH = to make someone or something completely wet

"We got caught in the rain and were DRENCHED when we got home."
"Your clothes are DRENCHED! Take them off and put on dry clothes."
"She DRENCHED the campfire with a bucket of water."

TO DROOL = 1. to let saliva flow from the mouth 2. to show admiration in an exaggerated way

"The baby is DROOLING. Wipe her mouth."
"The dog began to DROOL when I gave him a bone to chew."
"Everyone was DROOLING over his new truck."

DUMBFOUNDED = completely shocked or surprised

"We were DUMBFOUNDED to hear that he had died!"
"I'm DUMBFOUNDED to see you here! I didn't know you were back from Europe!"
"She was DUMBFOUNDED when her husband said he wanted a divorce."

TO DWINDLE = to gradually grow smaller or less

"The town's population is DWINDLING."
"The amount I owe will DWINDLE as I pay it off each month."
"My time is DWINDLING. I can stay only another minute or two."

e.

EAGER = very excited and interested

"I'm EAGER for the new class to begin."
"We're EAGER to see our new granddaughter!"
"Some of us are getting EAGER for spring. We're tired of winter."

EARNEST = serious and sincere

"She made an EARNEST plea for assistance."
"At first I thought he was joking, but then I realized he was being EARNEST."
"He's EARNEST in his beliefs. You won't change his mind."

TO EAVESDROP = to secretly listen to what someone is saying

"Kids, go away. I don't want you to EAVESDROP when I'm on the telephone."
"I'm sorry, I don't mean to EAVESDROP, but did I hear someone say my name?"
"It's not very nice to EAVESDROP. It might get you in trouble."

ECCENTRIC = acting in strange or unusual ways

"My ECCENTRIC neighbor wears an aluminum foil hat to keep mosquitoes away from him."
"He's a little ECCENTRIC, but he doesn't cause any trouble."
"She's becoming ECCENTRIC in her old age."

ECHO = a sound that is a copy of another sound

"Have you ever shouted in the mountains and heard the ECHO of your voice?"
"Be careful what you say to children. They might ECHO what you say."
"I'm getting an ECHO on my phone. Do you hear it, too?"

ECSTATIC = very happy or excited

"My dog was ECSTATIC to see me when I got home."
"The children are ECSTATIC because it's almost Christmas."
"We're ECSTATIC to be here! We think it will be a wonderful holiday!"

EDIBLE = able to be safely eaten

"Yes, the berries on that bush are EDIBLE."
"I mistakenly used salt instead of sugar. The result was not EDIBLE."
"The food was barely EDIBLE, but we didn't tell her."

TO EMBARRASS = to make someone feel foolish or uncomfortable

"She warned her husband not to drink too much and EMBARRASS her."
"I was EMBARRASSED when the class told me I forgot to zip my pants."
"The speaker was EMBARRASSED when the audience began to laugh."

TO EMBELLISH = to decorate something by adding details and features to make it more attractive

"She EMBELLISHED her outfit by adding a beautiful necklace."
"Just give me the facts. Don't EMBELLISH your story."
"The dress was EMBELLISHED with sequins and pearls."

TO EMPHASIZE = to give special attention to something; to stress the importance of something

"I cannot EMPHASIZE enough, if you want to learn English, you must study and practice."
"The teacher EMPHASIZED that the test would be very important."
"She EMPHASIZED that we would all be welcome at the party."

EMPIRE = a group of countries ruled by one person or government, or a large business controlled by one person or a company

"The Roman Empire lasted nearly 500 years."
"Nashville is the home of the country music EMPIRE."
"Did you see the Star Wars movie, *THE EMPIRE STRIKES BACK?*"

TO ENDURE = 1. to last or continue to exist
2. to deal with something unpleasan

"The Pyramids in Egypt have ENDURED for many centuries."
"I cannot ENDURE hard rock music."
"Nothing ENDURES forever."

TO ENGRAVE = to cut lines. letters, or designs on to a hard surface

"The inside of my wedding ring is ENGRAVED with our wedding date."
"The company gave him an ENGRAVED plaque when he retired."
"Your name is ENGRAVED in my memory. I will never forget you."

EPIDEMIC = an occurrence of disease or bad event which spreads quickly

"The flu EPIDEMIC of 1918 killed over 20 million people around the world."

"There was an EPIDEMIC of bank failures in 1930 that helped create the Great Depression in the United States."
"There seems to be an EPIDEMIC of crime in the city. The police are trying to stop it."

ERRATIC = not regular

"I have an ERRATIC heartbeat."
"Gasoline prices are very ERRATIC."
"The stock market has been ERRATIC the past few days."

ERRONEOUS = not correct

"It was an ERRONEOUS belief that the world is flat."
"They gave us ERRONEOUS information."
"The ERRONEOUS decision cost the company several thousand dollars."

TO EVACUATE = to remove someone from a dangerous place

"The forest fires in California caused many people to EVACUATE their homes."
"We had to EVACUATE the city when flooding began."
"How quickly can you EVACUATE the building?"

TO EXAGGERATE = to describe something as larger or greater than it really is

"Fishermen like to EXAGGERATE the size of the fish they catch."
"The company fired him because he EXAGGERATED his experience."
"The school EXAGGERATED how many students they served."

TO EXCEED = to be greater or more than something

"You're in trouble if your spending EXCEEDS your earnings."
"Be careful not to EXCEED the speed limit."

"The company's profits EXCEEDED what they expected."

EXCURSION = a short trip or a short outing

"We went on an EXCURSION to an exhibit in Columbus."
"His wife went on a shopping EXCURSION to New York City."
"Where would you like to go for our next EXCURSION?"

EXTENSIVE = large in size or amount

"The hurricanes caused EXTENSIVE damage in Puerto Rico."
"I took EXTENSIVE English classes in college."
"My daughter said she was in the shower and couldn't answer the phone. I tried to call for half an hour. It must have been an EXTENSIVE shower!"

EXTINCT = no longer existing

"Dinosaurs roamed the earth long ago, but now they are EXTINCT."
"Some people say that Latin is an EXTINCT language."
"If he doesn't slow down, he's going to be EXTINCT!"

EXTRAVAGANT = very fancy, or very expensive

"She bought an EXTRAVAGANT dress for her wedding."
"We celebrated our anniversary at an EXTRAVAGANT restaurant
"This is too EXTRAVAGANT. You shouldn't have done this!"

EXQUISITE = finely made, or very beautiful

"She wore an EXQUISITE diamond ring."
"It was an EXQUISITE performance."
'This has been an EXQUISITE evening. Thank you for inviting me!"

TO EVALUATE = to judge or rate something or someone in a careful way.

"We must EVALUATE the company before we buy it."
"How do you EVALUATE the class? Is it good or bad?"
"You should take that to be EVALUATED. It might be worth a lot of money."

f.

FALLACY = an incorrect belief

"It's a FALLACY that the company is moving to China."
"There's a FALLACY in your theory."
"His argument was full of FALLACIES,"

FAMINE = a situation in which people do not have enough food to eat

"During the Irish Potato FAMINE of 1845, many Irish people emigrated to the US."
"FAMINE is a problem in many parts of the world."
"We have to do what we can to help those experiencing FAMINE."

FANCY = not plain or ordinary

"He drives a FANCY car."
"She got a FANCY hairdo for her first date."
"I don't need anything FANCY. Something simple will be fine."

FEASIBLE = possible to do

"The company is looking for a FEASIBLE new location."
"It's not FEASIBLE to build a new hospital at this time."
"Let's consider all the possibilities and decide which is FEASIBLE."

FEEDBACK = information given to someone to offer an opinion on a performance, project or product

"I'd like your FEEDBACK on the class. What is good, what is bad, or what can be done to make it better?'

"Every year, the boss gives us FEEDBACK on our work."

"They didn't give us any FEEDBACK. I wonder what they think about it?"

FEUD = a long and angry fight between two people or two groups

"The Hatfield and McCoy FEUD is a famous fight between two families in the US."

"She's FEUDING with her husband, and she wants to stay here for a while."

"It's not worth FEUDING about it. Let's just forget about it."

TO FIDGET = to make small movements because you are nervous, bored, or restless

"Can you stop FIDGETING and just sit still?"

"It's hard to make children sit still. They begin to FIDGET after a while."

"Please don't FIDGET with the car window."

FIERCE = violent; eager to fight

"That man has a FIERCE dog. Stay away from it."

"It was a FIERCE battle."

"She has a FIERCE temper. Try not to make her angry."

FLAK = in wartime, FLAK is exploding shells shot at airplanes.
In slang today, FLAK is heavy criticism.

"He got a lot of FLAK from the other children because of his strange clothing."
"Don't give me any FLAK. Just do what I told you to do."
"My wife is giving me FLAK for not helping her enough."

FLAWED = having a mistake or weakness

"The shirt is on sale because it is FLAWED. The pockets are sown shut."
"The character Othello in Shakespeare's play had a FLAWED personality. He was overly jealous of his wife, Desdemona."
"This diamond is not the best. It is FLAWED with a couple small scratches."

FLUKE = an unexpected thing that happens by luck or accident

"Our team won, but it was a FLUKE. We could not do it again."
"I had not seen him for years. It was a FLUKE that we met in the grocery store."
"He was in a bad accident. It's just a FLUKE he wasn't killed."

FOE = enemy

"The US and Germany were FOES in World War I and World War II."
"Donald Trump and Hillary Clinton were FOES in the last Presidential election."
"HALT! Who goes there? Friend or FOE?"

FOOLHARDY = something that is dangerous or risky

"It's FOOLHARDY in winter to go outside without a coat."
"I lost all my money in a FOOLHARDY investment."

"Why do you want to do that? It sounds FOOLHARDY to me."

FOOTAGE = film or video recorded of some event

"I saw FOOTAGE of last week's football game."
"There was FOOTAGE on TV of Pope Francis' visit to Chile."
"Did you watch any FOOTAGE of the Olympic games?"

FOREHEAD = the part of the face above the eyes

"He has a scar on his FOREHEAD from an accident."
"I could see the sweat on his FOREHEAD."
"I bumped my FOREHEAD getting in the car."

TO FORFEIT = to lose something as a punishment, a rule, or a law

"He had to FORFEIT his driver's license to the police."
"He will FORFEIT his deposit if he doesn't return it on time."
"If your team doesn't have enough players, you will FORFEIT the game."

FOYER = the lobby or entryway to a building or house

"Let's meet in the FOYER of the library, then we will find a table we can use."
"Come into my FOYER and let me take your coat."
"The police found the victim lying in the FOYER."

FRACTURE = a crack or a break, especially as in a broken bone

"He FRACTURED his leg playing football."
"There's a FRACTURE in my basement wall."
"Water caused the wall to FRACTURE."

FRAGMENT = a broken part or piece of something

"There were FRAGMENTS of broken glass beneath the window."
ATE DINNER is a sentence FRAGMENT. "<u>Who</u> ate dinner?"
"The thieves didn't leave a FRAGMENT of evidence."

FRANTIC = feeling and showing fear and worry

"She was FRANTIC when she couldn't find her son."
"I was FRANTIC before my kids arrived home safely."
"Let's try to stay calm and not get FRANTIC."

FRAUD = 1. the crime of dishonesty, taking something valuable
2, a person who pretends to be what he or she is not

"He was guilty of bank FRAUD and was sent to prison."
"He claimed to be a doctor, but we learned that he was a FRAUD."
"She learned that her fiancé was a FRAUD who only wanted to
    marry her for her money."

FRECKLE = a small, brown spot on a person's skin

"He had FRECKLES on his face in the summertime."
"She was a pretty, redheaded girl with FRECKLES."
"Did you have FRECKLES when you were young?"

FRENZY = uncontrolled or wild activity

"She was in a FRENZY to get everything ready for the party."
"The day after Thanksgiving is a day of FRENZIED shopping for some
    people."
"The crowd worked itself into a FRENZY and attacked the building."

FROWN = a serious, disapproving expression, the opposite of a smile

"The teacher had a FROWN on her face."
"She FROWNED when she opened the letter."
"An upside down smile is a FROWN."

FRUGAL = using money or supplies very carefully

"We spent too much money last month. We have to be more FRUGAL."
"I try to be a FRUGAL shopper at the grocery store."
"We're almost out of coffee. Be FRUGAL with it until we go to the store."

FUNDAMENTAL = relating to the most important part or structure of something

"Food and water are FUNDAMENTALS of life."
"Let's get back to the FUNDAMENTALS of running our business."
"I took FUNDAMENTAL math when I was very young, and advanced math in high school."

FURIOUS = very angry

"My father was FURIOUS because I forgot to put gas in the car."
"Some people are FURIOUS with Donald Trump's policies."
"The man became FURIOUS and threatened to kill all of us."

FURTHERMORE = in addition to

"You're too young to go to Italy. FURTHERMORE, you don't speak Italian."
"I can't go out tonight. I'm too tired. FURTHERMORE, I don't have any money."
"You can't go out tonight. FURTHERMORE, you promised to help

me this evening."

FUSSY = hard to please; unhappy

"The baby is FUSSY, and I don't know what she wants."
"I'm not FUSSY about where we eat. Anyplace is fine with me."
"The kids have been FUSSY all day. I'll be glad when they go back to school."

FYI = the abbreviation for FOR YOUR INFORMATION

"FYI, that address is wrong. I have a new address.
"Yes, she's a beautiful woman, but FYI, she's married and not available."
"Oh, FYI, there's a note on the table for you."

g.

GALE = very strong wind

"There will be heavy snow and GALES tomorrow night."
"The boat came through some heavy GALES."
"The weather service is predicting GALE force winds of 70 to 80 km/h."

GATHER = to bring things or people together in a group

"Let's GATHER the apples that have fallen from the tree."
"We'll all GATHER at the library, then we'll go to lunch together."
"How many people GATHERED at the school?"

GENERATION = 1. the average time between parents and the birth of their children
2. the people born and living during the same time

"I'm the 4th GENERATION of my family in the US. My great-grandfather came here from Germany in 1853."
"The people of my GENERATION did not have computers and cell phones."
"It will be several GENERATIONS before people can live on the contaminated land."

TO GIGGLE = to laugh in a nervous or childlike way

"The children GIGGLED at the kittens playing."
"The girls were GIGGLING as the movie began."
"I told him a funny story, but I couldn't get a GIGGLE out of him."

GRADUAL = happening in a slow way over a period of time

"He has shown GRADUAL improvement after his surgery."
"There has been a GRADUAL increase in daylight since 21 December, the shortest day."
"The company is expecting a GRADUAL increase in sales."

GREGARIOUS = enjoying the company of other people

"Some students in class are quiet, and some are more GREGARIOUS."
"He does not enjoy parties. He is not very GREGARIOUS."
"She's quite GREGARIOUS. Everyone seems to like her."

TO GROUSE = to complain

"He GROUSES about his job. He doesn't like it very much."
"Kids, stop GROUSING about helping around the house. We all have to help."
"I'm tired of your GROUSING. Give it a rest!"

GRUMPY = having a bad temper; complaining

"The neighbor next door is always GRUMPY. Stay out of his yard."
"He woke up GRUMPY today. I hope he feels better later."
"You can't do anything about it. Quit being GRUMPY!"

> **GRAMMAR BREAK: BASIC COMMA RULES**
>
> Comma rules are most important in writing, and you should learn the rules.

In speaking, we often make a short pause where a comma would be used.
"In the springtime, the birds start to sing."
"John, bring your children with you."

Use a comma to separate 3 or more things in a series
"I went to the store and bought milk and eggs."
"I went to the store and bought milk, eggs, butter, and cheese."

Use a comma when the first word is YES or NO
"Yes, the school is closed today."
"No, I haven't seen him."

Use a comma between city and state
"I teach a class in Cleveland, Ohio."
note: do not use a comma if you abbreviate the state
'I teach a class in Cleveland OH."

Use a comma when you are directly addressing a person
"Maria, what's the answer to the first question?'
"What do you think, Ramona?"

Use a comma when writing out dates after the month and after the year
"He was born on January 14, 1980, in New York City."
note: do not use a comma if the date or the year is missing
"He was born on January 14 in New York City."
"He was born in 1980 in New York City."

Use a comma to separate independent clauses when they are joined by <u>and</u>, <u>but</u>, <u>for</u>, <u>or</u>, <u>nor</u>, <u>so</u>, or <u>yet</u>.
"<u>Sophia went to the store</u>, and <u>she bought milk</u>."
note: if NOT independent clauses, do not use a comma
"Sophia went to the store and bought milk."

Use a comma to separate a list of adjectives describing a subject
"The tall, skinny man is my father."
"The tall, skinny, bald, well dressed man is my father."

Use a comma to separate an introductory clause that comes before an independent clause
"When I missed the bus, I was late for work.."
note: when this clause comes after the independent clause do not use a comma
"I was late for work when I missed the bus."

Use a comma after an interrupting word like <u>HOWEVER</u> or <u>FURTHERMORE</u>
"I saw him at the bank. However, he didn't see me."
"She can't come out tonight. Furthermore, neither can her sister."

Use a comma after introductory words
"Sadly, the man died after his surgery."
"Finally, the letter arrived."

Use a comma to set off titles
"Robert Smith, MD, will speak to the class."

Use a comma around APPOSITIVES, clauses that do not change the sentence but add more information.
"Maria and Elizabeth, <u>who speak Spanish</u>, are in my class."
"Mr. Jones, <u>my next door neighbor</u>, is a school teacher."

Use commas before and after direct quotations
Mr. Bruce said, "Study and practice your English every day."

"Study and practice every day," he said, "if you want to speak better."

Use a comma to separate a comment from a question
"You speak Spanish, don't you?"

h.

HALF-BAKED = in slang, HALF-BAKED means not well planned or thought out.

"He has a HALF-BAKED plan to retire when he is 30 years old."
"The boss has some HALF-BAKED ideas to increase sales."
"I have some HALF-BAKED thoughts. Maybe one will work."

HANDFUL= 1. an amount that you can hold in your hand
2. a small number

"I washed a HANDFUL of grapes for your snack."
"There was a HANDFUL of people in the room."
"We saw a HANDFUL of cars in the parking lot, and we decided to stop."

HANGOVER = a sick feeling that comes after drinking too much alcohol

"He drank too much last night and has a HANGOVER this morning."
"Some people say that drinking tomato juice and avoiding coffee is a HANGOVER cure."
"HANGOVER or not, you can't stay home. You have to get up and go to work."

TO HARASS = to annoy or bother someone repeatedly

"Photographers sometimes HARASS famous people. Photographers who do this are called PAPARAZZI."
"The boss has been HARASSING me to finish, but I need a couple

more weeks."
"Don't HARASS him. It will only make him angry."

TO HEAD = to be going somewhere

"It's getting late. I'd better HEAD home."
"If you're HEADED to town, mail this letter for me."
"Can you drop me off at school when you HEAD to work?

HECTIC = very busy and filled with activity

"We had a HECTIC day at work today."
"I have a HECTIC schedule all week. Can I meet you next week?"
"This place is too HECTIC for me. Let's get out of here and go somewhere else."

HEREDITARY = passed from parent to child

"My blue eyes are HEREDITARY. Both my parents had blue eyes."
"His heart problems are HEREDITARY."
"What HEREDITARY traits do you have in you family?"

TO HESITATE = to stop briefly before you do something

"Don't HESITATE. This offer is good only today."
"He HESITATED until the cars were gone, then he crossed the street."
"She HESITATED too long, and she lost her opportunity."

TO HIBERNATE = to spend the winter sleeping

"Bears HIBERNATE over the winter."
"I'd like to HIBERNATE when the weather is cold!"
"I HIBERNATED in my room for almost two weeks to study for the exam."

HIGHFALUTIN' = an informal meaning someone who seems or tries to be important

"He has a HIGHFALUTIN' way of speaking that I don't like."
"The concert attracted a lot of HIGHFALUTIN' people."
"I went to a HIGHFALUTIN' party. All the women wore formal dresses, and all the men wore tuxedos."

TO HINDER = to make something as a job or project slow or difficult

"Our plan to create jobs is HINDERED by a lack of money."
"The job was HINDERED because there was no electricity."
"Get it done. Don't let anything HINDER you."

HOARSE = unable to speak clearly because of a rough voice

"I shouted too much yesterday, and today I am HOARSE."
"I've had a cold, and I am still HOARSE."
"My wife often got HOARSE teaching a music class."

HOMELY = not pretty or handsome

"He's HOMELY, but he has a nice personality."
"She has a HOMELY face."
"Abraham Lincoln grew a beard because a little girl told him he was HOMELY without it."

HORRIFIED = greatly upset and shocked

"I was HORRIFIED to see the man beating his wife."
"Aren't you HORRIFIED by the shootings in our schools?"
"We were all HORRIFIED by the terrible accident."

TO HUMILIATE = to make someone feel ashamed

"He drank too much at the party and HUMILIATED his wife."
"The other team won by 50 points. It was a HUMILIATING defeat for us."
"I could never do that. It would HUMILIATE ME."

HUNCH(noun)= a belief about something
(verb)= to bend your body forward so that your back is rounded

"They were HUNCHED over the table to see the map."
"It's good to see you. I had a HUNCH you'd be here today."
"If you're not sure of the answer to the question, use your best HUNCH."

HUSKY = large and strong

"I was always HUSKY when I was in school."
"The workers were all HUSKY men."
"There's a breed of dog that is also called a 'HUSKY.'"

HYPOTHETICAL = not real; used as an example

"It's a HYPOTHETICAL question. What would you do with a million dollars?"
"Speaking HYPOTHETICALLY, would you do it?"
"What would you do if...is a HYPOTHETICAL game."

HYSTERICAL = 1. showing extreme and uncontrollable emotion

"She became HYSTERICAL when told that her son had been killed."

HYSTERICAL = 2. very, very funny

"It was a HYSTERICAL movie. We couldn't stop laughing."

i.

TO ILLUSTRATE = to give or show examples to make something easier to understand

"Some grammar rules are easier to understand if I ILLUSTRATE them."
"Give me some examples to ILLUSTRATE your idea."
"He drew pictures on the board to ILLUSTRATE his explanation."

IMPARTIAL = judging fairly without being influenced by either side

"Judges in the court must be IMPARTIAL and consider only the facts."
"I cannot be IMPARTIAL in this case. The defendant is my brother."
"We need to talk to someone who will listen to our problems and give us IMPARTIAL advice."

TO IMPEDE = to slow the movement, progress, or action of someone or something

"I know you are in a hurry. I won't IMPEDE you."
"My trip home was IMPEDED by heavy traffic."
"Don't let anything IMPEDE you. Get the job done quickly."

IMPETUOUS = acting or done quickly without thought

"It was an IMPETUOUS purchase."
"He made an IMPETUOUS decision to quit his job."

"They've only known each other a few weeks. Getting married now is IMPETUOUS."

INCOMPETENT = lacking ability and skills

"The salesman was INCOMPETENT. He couldn't answer our questions."
"Do you think Donald Trump is an INCOMPETENT President?"
"We can't keep INCOMPETENT workers."

TO INDICATE = to show or direct attention to, or to state briefly

"The thermometer INDICATES that it is 4 degrees C."
"Please INDICATE your country on the map."
"She INDICATED that she would be here next week."

INDIFFERENT = 1. not interested or caring about something
2. not very good

"The people were INDIFFERENT about the election."
"Was the food good, bad, or INDIFFERENT?"
"I'm INDIFFERENT. It doesn't matter to me, one way or the other."

INDIVIDUAL = relating to one person or part of something

"Teachers must consider the needs of each INDIVIDUAL student."
"Three INDIVIDUALS were given the award."
"I saw an INDIVIDUAL go into the store."

INEVITABLE = sure to happen

"Some people like to say that only death and taxes are INEVITABLE."
"Other people joke it's INEVITABLE that if something can go wrong, it will."

"If I'm late to work just once, it's INEVITABLE that the boss will see me.

INMATE = a person kept in prison

"The American gangster Al Capone was an INMATE at Alcatraz Federal Penitentiary."
"The INMATES escaped, but they were re-captured by the police."
"The INMATES started a riot in the cafeteria."

INNOVATION = a new idea, product, or method

"What do you think is the greatest INNOVATION this century?"
"There have been a lot of INNOVATIONS in computers."
"Have there been any INNOVATIONS in your line of work?"

INSECURE = 1. not confident or sure about your abilities
2. not locked

"She felt shy and INSECURE with other people."
"The back door of the building was INSECURE."
"I'm INSECURE about the house. Did we lock the door or not?"

INTENTIONAL = on purpose, or done in a way that was planned

"His reason for doing it was INTENTIONAL."
"I'm sorry I hurt you. It was not INTENTIONAL."
"The bombing of Pearl Harbor was an INTENTIONAL act of war."

TO INTERJECT = to interrupt what someone else is saying to add a comment

"I heard you talking; let me INTERJECT something."
"Have you thought about the cost?" he INTERJECTED.
"Please don't INTERJECT while i am talking. Save any questions

until I am finished."

TO INTRUDE = to come or go into a place where you are not wanted

"I'm sorry to INTRUDE on your meeting, but the boss needs to take a phone call."
"Please don't INTRUDE on our conversation."
"A man INTRUDED into the women's restroom by mistake."

INTUITION = a feeling that guides us to act a certain way without knowing why

"Trust your INTUITION and do what you think is best."
"Some people say that a mother's INTUITION is a superpower."
"My INTUITION tells ne that we ought to get out of here."

TO INUNDATE = 1. to cause someone to take in a large number of things at the same time
2. to cover something with water

"The police station was INUNDATED with phone calls about the robbery."
"We have been INUNDATED by four days of rain."
"I'm INUNDATED with work today. There's no way I'll be home early."

INVOICE = a bill showing a list of materials or goods and the prices to be paid for them

"The INVOICE was included in the shipping box"
"I'll send you an INVOICE for the work I have done."
"She can't find the INVOICE. Have you seen it?"

TO IRK = to bother or annoy someone

"It IRKS me when you borrow the car but don't put any gas in it"

"It IRKS my wife when the TV is too loud."
"I can never find a pen in this house. That IRKS me!"

> **TO IRRIGATE** =1. **to bring water to dry land through pipes**
> 2. *medical* **to clean a wound with water**

"He IRRIGATED his land to grow more wheat."
"Would it help to try to IRRIGATE the field?"
"The doctor IRRIGATED the cut on his arm."

JARGON = the language used for particular activity or by a particular group of people

"Medical JARGON is difficult to understand."
"He's very good at speaking sports JARGON."
"Once you learn the JARGON, you'll do fine."

JERK(verb) = a quick pull

"She JERKED me out of the way of the speeding car."
"Someone JERKED my arm, and I spilled my coffee."

JERK(noun) = a person who is not well liked or who treats people badly

"Don't go out with him. He's a JERK."
"Some JERK parked too close to me. I can't open my door."

k.

TO KIDNAP = to take someone by force to keep as a prisoner and to demand money for returning the person.

"Be careful not to let anyone KIDNAP the baby!"
"You can go to the prison for more than 20 years if you KIDNAP someone."

KINDHEARTED = having or showing a kind and gentle nature

"A KINDHEARTED driver stopped and helped me change a tire."
"My neighbor is a KINDHEARTED woman."

KIN = relatives

"I have KIN living in Kentucky."
"We have the same last name, but we are not KIN."

KNOT [silent "k"; sounds like "not] = 1) a part that forms when you tie a rope or string to itself or something else

"She tied the rope in a KNOT."
"There's a KNOT in my shoelaces."

2) a painful feeling or tightness in part of your body

"I have a KNOT in my leg muscle."
"I was so nervous that I felt KNOTS in my stomach."

1.

LATE = 1. not on time

"I was LATE for class today."
"Don't be LATE again."

LATE = 2. no longer living

"The LATE Mr. Smith was my favorite teacher."
"The LATE President KENNEDY was born in 1917."

LECTURE = a talk or speech given to a group of people to teach them about a subject

"I attended a LECTURE about the history of Ohio."
"She's planning to give a LECTURE about her country."
"Did you take notes at the LECTURE?'

LEECH = 1. a kind of worm that attaches itself to the skin and sucks blood

"He went swimming in the river. When he came out, a LEECH was attached to his leg."

2. a person who takes from others without giving anything in return

"My college roommate was a LEECH. He never gave us money for food or expenses."
"He's a LEECH living off his family and friends. I don't think he's ever had a job."

LENIENT = not strict

"Some parents are too LENIENT with their children."
"My best teachers in school were strict, not LENIENT."

LIMP(verb) = to walk slowly because of a leg or foot injury
(adjective) = not firm or stiff

"She sprained her ankle and had to LIMP to the car."
"Why are you LIMPING?"
"Her knees went LIMP when she heard the bad news."
"He gave me a LIMP handshake."

LISTLESS = lacking energy or spirit

"It was a LISTLESS summer day, not even a breeze was blowing in the trees."
"I feel LISTLESS today. I don't want to do anything."
"It was a LISTLESS party until the band arrived."

LOPSIDED = not straight or even

"The picture on the wall is LOPSIDED. Can you straighten it, please?"
"The table is LOPSIDED. One leg is too short."
"It was a LOPSIDED game. One team didn't score a point."

LOUSY = bad or poor; of poor quality

"He got LOUSY grades in school."
"The workers did a LOUSY job."
"I feel LOUSY today. I think I'll not go to work."

LULL = a break in action or activity

"We've been busy all day without even a LULL."

"There was a LULL in the conversation when no one said anything."
"There was a LULL in the game when the injured player was carried off the field."

> **GRAMMAR BREAK: USING EITHER and NEITHER**
>
> We usually use EITHER and NEITHER when we are talking about a choice of two things. We use EITHER to indicate one of a group or two, and we use NEITHER to indicate not one of the group of two.

"I have two boys. EITHER can help you cut your grass."
"Both boys are working. NEITHER can help you cut your grass.

EITHER is used in positive statements, and **NEITHER** is used in negative statements."

"Do you want tea or coffee?" "EITHER is fine. I'll have what you are having."
"Do you want tea or coffee?" "NEITHER. Bring me a bottle of beer."
"Both sweaters are pretty. EITHER will look nice on you."
"One is too big, the other is too small. NEITHER will fit me."

We use **OR** with **EITHER**, and we use **NOR** with **NEITHER**.

"EITHER Maria OR Ramona can help you with your Spanish."
"NEITHER Maria NOR Ramona speaks Japanese."

We also combine **EITHER / OR** and **NEITHER / NOR** to offer a choice between two things.

"I'll EITHER call you OR send you an email tonight."
"EITHER your sister OR your brother can help you with your homework."
"NEITHER call me NOR send me an email.. I won't be home tonight.."
"NEITHER your sister NOR your brother will be here to help you."

We sometimes use **EITHER** and **NEITHER** as linking words.

"I don't like Brussel sprouts."
"NEITHER do I."
"She doesn't drink soft drinks."
"I don't drink them, EITHER."

m.

MALARKEY = foolish words or ideas

"She's telling you a lot of MALARKEY. Don't believe a word of it."
"What the politicians tell us is nothing but MALARKEY."
"He tried to tell me why he was late, but it was just MALARKEY."

TO MALIGN = to say bad words about someone or something

"I quit my job, and now my old boss is MALIGNING me."
"Many people like to MALIGN the President."
"Please don't MALIGN my work. I'm doing the best that I can."

MANDATORY = required by a law or rule

"It's MANDATORY for all essential employees to come to work today."
"The meeting is MANDATORY. Everyone must attend."
"The company has a MANDATORY drug test for all employees."

TO MAUL = to attack or injure someone

"The dog MAULED the woman to death."
"After a dog has MAULED someone, it should be taken away."
"His hand was MAULED in the machinery."

TO MEANDER = to walk aimlessly; not in a straight line; without any direction

"We spent the afternoon MEANDERING through the mall."

"The river MEANDERS through the state."
"Our conversation MEANDERED over several topics."

MEANWHILE = at or during the same time

"I cleaned the living room. MEANWHILE, my wife worked in the kitchen."
"You go to the grocery store. MEANWHILE, we'll go to the post office, then we'll come back to meet you."
"We were coming in the front door. MEANWHILE, the thieves were running out the backdoor."

TO MEDDLE = to give unwanted involvement to other peoples' activities or affairs

"I have a nosy neighbor who MEDDLES in everyone's personal lives."
"Please don't MEDDLE in my room while I am away."
"Stay out of it. Don't MEDDLE."

MEMENTO = something kept as a reminder of a person, place, or thing

"My hat is a MEMENTO of my trip to Ecuador."
"That table is a MEMENTO from my mother's house."
"When you come home, bring me a MEMENTO."

MEMO = shortened form of MEMORANDUM, a brief written note from one person or organization or office to another person or office

"The boss sent us a MEMO about the meeting next week."
"Send a MEMO to accounting and ask them for our latest expenses."
"Have you seen the latest MEMO?"

MEMORABLE = easily remembered

"What the most MEMORABLE thing from your vacation?"
"President Kennedy's assassination is a MEMORABLE event in my life."
"We took a very MEMORABLE vacation to Germany."

TO MEND = to fix or repair

"It will take time for your broken arm to MEND."
"We had a fight. Can we MEND our friendship?"
"Take it to the shop. Maybe they can MEND it."

MIFFED = upset or annoyed

"She's MIFFED because I didn't call her."
"They were MIFFED that they didn't receive an invitation."
"Will they be MIFFED if we don't go?"

MILEAGE = distance in miles

"What's the MILEAGE between Chicago and Los Angeles?"
"My old car has a lot of MILEAGE on it."
"The old man said there's a lot of MILEAGE on his body."

TO MINE (verb) = to dig in the ground for coal, gold, diamonds, and so on

"In 1850, many people went to California to MINE for gold."

MINE (PRONOUN) = that which belongs to me

"That coat is MINE."

MINE (noun) = a hole or tunnel in the ground for bringing out coal, gold, diamonds, and so on

"My cousin works in a coal MINE in Kentucky."

MISSPELL = to spell incorrectly

"Some Americans MISSPELL this word. They forget the double "s.""
"Frantz? No, you've MISSPELLED my name. There's no 't' in Franz."
"It's easy to MISSPELL some words. That's why we have dictionaries."

TO MODIFY = to change part of something

"I MODIFIED the recipe by using less sugar."
"Can you MODIFY the list and add my name to it?"
"This can't be MODIFIED. You'll have to buy a new one."

MODULAR = having parts that can be connected or combined

"We had MODULAR furniture in the office where I worked."
"While looking for a house, we also looked at a factory that made MODULAR homes."
" I wonder what the next product to go MODULAR will be?"

MONITOR (noun) = a device for showing, watching, or listening to something

"They have a baby MONITOR to hear when he wakes up."
"I had to wear a heart MONITOR for a week."
"My computer MONITOR isn't working."

TO MONITOR (verb) = to watch, listen, or observe something

"The teacher will MONITOR your progress in the class."
"MONITOR his temperature and call us if there is a change."

MOONLIGHT = yes, MOONLIGHT is the light you see from the moon

"Her hair looked beautiful in the MOONLIGHT"

but the verb TO MOONLIGHT means to work a second job

"I was a salesman during the week, but on weekends I MOONLIGHTED in a department store."
"If you want extra cash, you might try MOONLIGHTING somewhere."

MORALE = the feeling of enthusiasm and loyalty that a worker or group has for the task or job to be done

"Employee MORALE is low. They haven't had a raise in pay for three years."
"The President hasn't done much to raise the MORALE of the voters."
"Good MORALE is as important as good wages."

MORGUE = a place where dead bodies are kept until they are buried or cremated

"I've never been in a MORGUE. I wonder what it would be like to work there?"
"His body was taken to the MORGUE until he could be identified."

figuratively = "This place is as quiet as a MORGUE."

MORSEL = a small piece of food

"I ate the cake and didn't leave a MORSEL."
"Use your napkin. You have a MORSEL of spinach between your teeth."
"Sample this MORSEL. Is it OK, or does it need anything?"

MUDSLIDE = large mass of wet earth that suddenly slides down the side of a mountain or hill

"Some people in California had to leave their homes because of

MUDSLIDES."
"Sadly, some people were killed in the MUDSLIDES."
"The MUDSLIDES swept away trees, cars, and homes."

MUGGY = unpleasantly hot and humid

"Hot summer days can be MUGGY as well."
"On MUGGY days I feel like I need to take a shower twice a day."
"Let's stay in today. It's too MUGGY outside."

MURKY = very dark or foggy; not clear

"The water was clear yesterday, but it's MURKY today."
"You can't see well to drive if the weather is MURKY."
"His work experience is rather MURKY."

n.

NEUROTIC = always feeling fearful or worried about something

"My mother didn't like airplanes. She felt NEUROTIC when her son had to fly in an airplane."
"She is NEUROTIC about keeping the windows clean."
"If he gets too NEUROTIC, he may have to take medication to calm him down."

NEVERTHELESS = in spite of what has just been said

"The traffic is heavy; NEVERTHELESS, he plans to come."
"She was 20 minutes late; NEVERTHELESS, he decided to keep waiting."

TO NICK = to make a small cut, or to damage a small part of the surface of something

"I NICKED my face while I was shaving."
"The bullet didn't hit him, but it NICKED his shoulder."
"Be careful not to NICK the table with your keys."

NIL = nothing or not at all

"The chances for rain today are NIL.
"He knows NIL about it."
"She had NIL to say."

NOGGIN = a person's head

"The baby fell and bumped his NOGGIN on the table."
"Use your NOGGIN and figure it out."
"Watch your NOGGIN as you get in the car."

NOOSE = a loop at the end of a rope that gets smaller when you pull the rope

"They put his head in a NOOSE and hanged him."
"The animal stepped in the NOOSE and was trapped."
"Put a NOOSE around the horse's neck and bring him into the barn."

NOTION = an idea or opinion, or an idea about doing something

"He has some strange NOTIONS."
"I have a NOTION to call my brother tonight."
"We don't have a NOTION where he is."

TO NOURISH = to provide someone or something with food, water, and so on to live and be healthy

"You have to NOURISH the flowers if you want them to grow."
"I take vitamins to NOURISH my body."
"She likes the piano. If we NOURISH that interest, she might become a great pianist."

NOVICE = a beginner; a person who has just started learning or doing something

"He's a NOVICE chess player."
"We need to hire someone with experience, not a NOVICE."
"I'm just a NOVICE, but I hope I'll get better."

NUGGET =1. a small piece of a valuable metal

"The miner came down from the mountain with a small bag of gold NUGGETS."

2. a small, round piece of food

"Have you tried chicken NUGGETS at the fast food restaurant?"

3. a piece of information

"I read the advice columnist's NUGGETS in the newspaper."

NUMEROUS = many, or a large number

"I have told you NUMEROUS times to lock the door when you leave."

"She has NUMEROUS friends on Facebook."

"The shop sells NUMEROUS different items."

O.

OBJECT = a thing that you can see and touch

"What OBJECTS do you have in your purse?"
"I keep several OBJECTS in my car."
"Did you see that OBJECT on the road?'

TO OBJECT = to disagree with something or oppose something

"No one OBJECTED when the tree was cut down."
"I OBJECT to same sex marriages."
"Does anyone OBJECT if I sit here?"

OBLIVIOUS = not conscious or aware of something

"I called to him, but he was OBLIVIOUS and didn't hear me."
"She kept talking, OBLIVIOUS that no one was listening."
"They were OBLIVIOUS to what was going on around them."

TO OBSERVE = to watch, or see, or listen to someone or something

"I OBSERVED the squirrels running around the yard."
"Did you OBSERVE anyone on the street last night?"
"We OBSERVED a moving truck in their driveway."

OBSOLETE = no longer used by anyone

"The first computer that I bought 20 years ago is OBSOLETE today."
"Some people say that Latin is an OBSOLETE language."

"Change is happening so quickly that what's new today will be OBSOLETE tomorrow!"

OBSTACLE = something blocking your path, or something that makes it difficult to do something

"I saw an OBSTACLE in the road, and I swerved my car to get around it."
"He had to overcome many OBSTACLES before he could succeed."
"Price is no OBSTACLE to him."

TO OBTAIN = to get something

"Where can I go to OBTAIN a passport?"
"Have you OBTAINED your American citizenship yet?"
"That can't be OBTAINED in the US."

OBVIOUS = easy to see or notice

"Your accent makes it OBVIOUS that you are French."
"It's OBVIOUS that you are lost. Can I help you?"
"It's not OBVIOUS to me."

OCCASIONAL = not happening in a regular way

"I have an OCCASIONAL glass of wine with dinner."
"OCCASIONAL rain showers are predicted for tomorrow."
"She takes an OCCASIONAL trip to visit her daughter."

OFFHAND = without previous thought or preparation

"How many people were there? OFFHAND, I would guess maybe 100 people."
"OFFHAND, he may be home about 4:00 or 4:30."
"It was an OFFHAND remark. It wasn't important."

OODLES = a large amount of something

"He's a rich man. He has OODLES of money."
"There was OODLES of food at the party."
"I lifted up the rock, and OODLES of bugs started running away."

TO OPT = to choose one thing instead of another

"I OPTED to go to Paris this year instead of London."
"Did he OPT to go to college, or to take the job?"
"We OPTED not to order dessert at the restaurant."

OPTIMIST = a person who expects good things to happen

"An OPTIMIST sees the best in everything."
"I lost my job, my wife left me, my car won't start....how can I be an OPTIMIST?"
"It's hard to be an OPTIMIST when so many things are bad!"

OUTCOME = the results of an activity or process

"What was the OUTCOME of last night's game?"
"The OUTCOME of the meeting will be announced tomorrow."
"I don't know what the OUTCOME will be."

TO OUTGROW = 1. to grow too large for something

"It doesn't take long for children to OUTGROW their clothes."

2. to stop doing something because you are older

"He's going through a phase. I hope he OUTGROWS it soon."

OVERALL = as a whole, or in general

"She missed a few questions, but she did well OVERALL."
"OVERALL, it was a great vacation."
"We had some losses, but it has been a good year OVERALL."

OVERALLS = a pair of pants with an extra piece attached that covers the chest and has two straps to go over the shoulders

"Some men wear OVERALLS to go to work."
"He wears a clean pair of OVERALLS every day."

TO OVERHEAR = to hear by accident something that was said to another person

"I was in the restroom and OVERHEARD the boss tell someone that he was going to retire."
"If you OVERHEAR anything about it, please let me know."
"Did you OVERHEAR the argument we had last night?"

TO OVERSEE = to watch and direct a worker or group of workers to be sure the work is done properly

"I want you to OVERSEE the new employee until we are sure he is capable."
"They hired me to OVERSEE the construction project."
"We need someone to OVERSEE the new office."

p.

PALACE = the official home of a king or queen; or a very large and impressive home

"Have you ever visited Buckingham Palace in London?"
"The rich man built himself a PALACE on top of the hill."
"We have more amenities in our homes today than PALACES had in the past."

PALATE = the top part of the inside of your mouth; also the sense of taste

"Sometimes babies are born with a split PALATE that must be repaired."
"My wife does not have the PALATE for hot, spicy foods."
"How does that suit your PALATE?"

PAMPHLET = a small booklet with no cover or only a paper cover with information about a particular subject

"I picked up a PAMPHLET at the library about ESL classes in Cleveland."
"She ordered 1000 PAMPHLETS about the festival."
"The PAMPHLET describes the services offered at the bank."

PANHANDLER = a person who asks strangers for money in a public place

"When I visited Germany, there were sometimes PANHANDLERS at the train stations."
"PANHANDLERS are not allowed in some cities."

"The PANHANDLER asked me if I had any change."

TO PARALYZE = to make a person or animal unable to move or feel part of the body

"The motorcycle accident PARALYZED him from the neck down."
"His legs are PARALYZED, and he must use a wheelchair."
"The deer stood PARALYZED in the headlights of my car."

PARODY = a piece of writing, music, or so on that imitates something else in a humorous way

"A common poem in the US is: Roses are red, Violets are blue, Sugar is sweet, and so are you."
"A PARODY of this is: Noses are red, Fingers are blue. I'm tired of winter, How about you?"
"He sang a PARODY of Elvis Presley songs."

PASTURE = a large area of land where animals feed on grain

"The cows are in the PASTURE."
"Take the horses to the PASTURE and let them graze."
"Most of his farm is in PASTURE."

PEDIATRICIAN = a doctor who treats babies and children

"My 2-year-old daughter has an appointment with the PEDIATRICIAN."
"It takes about eleven years of school and training to become a PEDIATRICIAN."
"The PEDIATRICIAN told us not to worry about anything."

PEDOPHILE = a person who has a sexual interest in children

"The police arrested a PEDOPHILE near the school."
"PEDOPHILES may be sent to prison if they are seen bothering children."
"You can check the computer to see if there are any PEDOPHILES in your neighborhood."

PENSIVE = quietly thoughtful

"She drank her coffee slowly, watching the children play and looking PENSIVE."
"She looked PENSIVE, so I asked her what was she thinking."
"He's a PENSIVE young writer working on his first book."

PERSISTENT = continuing to do something, or to keep trying to do something even though it is difficult

"There was a PERSISTENT knock at the door."
"If you are PERSISTENT about looking for a job, I'm sure you will find one."
"The salesman was very PERSISTENT to sell us a new car."

PERSPECTIVE = a way of thinking about something

"What's your PERSPECTIVE on Donald Trump? Is he doing a good job?"
"From my PERSPECTIVE, your position is weak and needs more thought."
"Learn more about it, and you might have a different PERSPECTIVE."

TO PERSPIRE = to produce clear liquid from your skin when you are hot; to sweat

"I begin to PERSPIRE in hot, humid weather."

"The man PERSPIRED when the police questioned him."
"He works in a hot place that causes him to PERSPIRE a lot."

TO PERSUADE = 1. to cause someone to do something by asking, arguing, or giving reasons

"He PERSUADED me to go with him."

2. to cause someone to believe something

"She PERSUADED us that we were mistaken."

PESSIMIST = a person who usually expects bad things to happen

"A PESSIMIST thinks everything is wrong with the world."
"Stop being such a PESSIMIST. Can't you see the bright side of things?"
"Murphy's Law says that if anything can go wrong, it will. Murphy was a PESSIMIST."

TO PLAGIARIZE = to use the words or ideas of another person

"Do you think Shakespeare PLAGIARIZED any of his works?"
"He PLAGIARIZED his report from another student."
"PLAGIARIZING will not be permitted in my class."

PLEDGE = a serious promise or agreement

"In court, they may ask you to give your PLEDGE that you will tell the truth."
If you become a US citizen, you must give a PLEDGE to be a good citizen."
"Give me your PLEDGE that you won't do it again."

PODIUM = a raised platform for a speaker, performer, or music conductor

"The President stood behind the PODIUM and spoke to the people."
"Some teachers like to use a PODIUM, and some don't."
"We all applauded when he stepped up to the PODIUM."

TO polish = to make something shiny by rubbing it

"My father wants me to POLISH the car every week."
"I need to POLISH my shoes."

Polish = a person from Poland

"Pope John Paul II was Polish."
"The Polish ambassador will speak to President Trump."

TO POSTPONE = to delay something that had been planned for a specific date

"We had to POSTPONE our picnic because of the rain."
"There will be no class today. It has been POSTPONED until next week."
"The delivery has been POSTPONED again. Now they say it will be next week."

TO POUNCE = to jump suddenly toward something

"The cat POUNCED on the toy mouse."
"All the children tried to POUNCE on the ball."
"Kids, please don't POUNCE on me when I come home."

TO POUR = to cause something to flow in a stream into another container

"Please POUR water into all the glasses."

"Can I POUR you another cup of coffee?"
"The rain is POURING down today."

TO POUT = to push out your lips to show that you are angry or disappointed

"The little boy POUTED when he dropped his ice cream."
"The girl POUTED and began to cry."
"Don't POUT. Everything will be OK."

PRECAUTION = something done to prevent harm or trouble from beginning

"Please take every PRECAUTION to keep yourself safe."
"You should always use a seatbelt as a PRECAUTION."
"Let's take PRECAUTIONS that this won't happen again."

PRECINCT = one of the sections that a city is divided into where people vote, or for organizing the city's police force

"I vote in the city's 5th PRECINCT."
"The PRECINCTS for voting will be open from 6:00 AM to 7:00 PM."
"His son is a policeman in the 18th PRECINCT."

PRECISE = very accurate and exact

"I've checked the numbers twice. Everything is PRECISE."
"Take a PRECISE measurement of the table."
"The plates and silverware must be PRECISE."

TO PREDICT = to say that something will or might happen in the future

"The weather report PREDICTS rain tomorrow."
"Did you PREDICT that Hillary Clinton would win the election, or
    Donald Trump?"

"I can't PREDICT what he might do."

TO PROCEED = to continue to do something, or to move in a particular direction

"The policeman motioned for us to PROCEED."
"The people PROCEEDED toward the door."
"We can't PROCEED without his approval."

PUSHY = using forceful methods to make others do what you want; aggressive

"The PUSHY salesman tried to make us buy it."
"The woman got PUSHY when I told her she couldn't come in."
"Don't get PUSHY with me!"

> **GRAMMAR BREAK: PAST TENSE SOUNDS**
>
> Past tense verbs can be pronounced with a "-t" sound, with a "-d" sound, or with an "-id" sound.

Following are the rules for making past tense sounds. No one I know uses these rules. We learn the words as we learn to speak. I suggest you do the same! Learn the pronunciation of words as you learn new vocabulary!

In the first group, if the sound of the verb ends in a voiceless sound of p, k, s, ch, sh, f, x, or h, the past tense "-ed" will sound like "-t."

CHOPPED	WASHED
ESCAPED	PUSHED
ASKED	LAUGHED
COOKED	COUGHED
DRESSED	MIXED
GUESSED	RELAXED
WATCHED	FINISHED
PATCHED	POLISHED

In the second group, if the sound of the verb ends in a voiced sound of l, v, n, m, r, b, g, w, y, z, or a vowel sound, the past "-ed" will sound like "-d."

CALLED	BELONGED
PULLED	DAMAGED
LOVED	SHOWED

MOVED	ALLOWED
OPENED	PLAYED
RAINED	STAYED
WELCOME	DFIZZED
PERFORMED	REALIZED
POURED	CRIED
MEASURED	AGREED
RUBBED	
SUBBED	

in the third group, if the verb ends in a "-t" or "-d" sound then the past tense "-ed" will sound like "-id."

COLLECTED	DECIDED
COUNTED	ENDED
HATED	INCLUDED
INVITED	NEEDED
RENTED	DEMANDED
RESTED	PADDED

q.

QUAINT = attractively unusual or old-fashioned

"We visited some QUAINT German restaurants in Berlin"
"The Amish people in the US have some QUAINT customs."
"The elderly man was dressed in a QUAINT old suit."

TO QUIT = to stop something, or to leave a job, school, activity or so on

"I QUIT smoking in 1980." "He QUIT school and got a job."
"We QUIT working at 9:00 PM last night."

QUITE = very

"It's getting QUITE late. We should be getting home."
"She is a QUITE beautiful woman." "It's QUITE cold today."

QUIET = not talking; making no noise; not having much activity

"Be QUIET," the teacher said.
"The room was QUIET."
"Business at the store was QUIET today."

r.

TO REACT = to change or behave in a certain way to something said, or to what happens

"How did he REACT when you told him? Was he angry?"
"The police REACTED quickly to the alarm."
"She REACTED by slapping me in the face!"

TO RECALL = to remember

"Do you RECALL the time we spent in Cleveland?"
"I'm sorry, I don't RECALL his name."
"Were we in the same class? Do you RECALL?"

RECKLESS = not showing concern about the possible bad effects of your actions

"I don't like to ride with him. He's a RECKLESS driver."
"I was a RECKLESS young man, but I have changed."
"Be careful! Don't do anything RECKLESS!"

RECTANGULAR = a shape of two pairs of parallel lines and four right angles

"A RECTANGULAR rug would look nice in this room."
"My friend has a RECTANGULAR jaw."
"The mailman delivered a RECTANGULAR box. What's in it?"

TO RECUPERATE = to get better after an illness, accident, or so on

"I'm not sure he can RECUPERATE."
"I was sick last week, but I am beginning to RECUPERATE."
"After his surgery, he needed time to RECUPERATE."

TO REGISTER = to put your name on an official list

"When an American is 18 years old, he or she can REGISTER to vote"
"Monday is the last day to REGISTER for class."
"Where do we have to go to REGISTER?"

TO REITERATE = to repeat or say again for emphasis

"I cannot REITERATE enough, you must study and practice to learn English."
"She REITERATED several times to bring our books."
"Before you go. let me REITERATE one more time, there is no class tomorrow!"

TO REJECT = to refuse to accept, believe, or consider something

"The boss REJECTED my idea."
"He asked her to marry him, but she REJECTED his proposal."
"The bank REJECTED our loan application."

RELEVANT = relating to a subject in an important way

"The class asked RELEVANT questions about the lesson."
"Personal questions are not RELEVANT in a job interview."
"She has RELEVANT work experience. I think we should hire her."

RELIC = something from a past time, place, or culture

"They dug into the earth and found RELICS from an earlier settlement."
"I have some tools that are RELICS from my grandfather's farm."
"We saw RELICS from King Tutankhamun's tomb in the museum."

RELUCTANT = not eager or willing to do something

"I'm RELUCTANT to tell her the bad news."
"He was RELUCTANT to go with me."
"The hospital is RELUCTANT to send him home yet."

TO REMEMBER = to have or keep in your mind something or someone from your past

"Do you REMEMBER your very first teacher?"
"I don't REMEMBER my grandfather. He died when I was a baby."
"Please REMEMBER to call me when you get there."

TO REMINISCE = to remember and talk or write about things in your past

"We had our 50th class reunion. It was fun to REMINISCE with others about our experience."
"My wife and I REMINISCE about the time we spent in Germany."
"The old man likes to REMINISCE about his youth."

TO RENOVATE = to change or remodel a room, a house, a building, and so on

"My wife wants to RENOVATE our kitchen."
"They bought an old house and RENOVATED it."
"The city doesn't have the money to RENOVATE the old building, so they plan to tear it down and make a parking lot."

TO REPRIMAND = to speak in a critical way to someone who has done something wrong

"The boss REPRIMANDED us for taking an extra long lunch break"
"We have to REPRIMAND the employees for parking in front of the building."
"I hope you won't REPRIMAND me. I did what I thought was best."

TO RESEMBLE = to look like something or someone else

"Many people say that my brothers and I RESEMBLE each other."
"I bought a clock that RESEMBLES one I used to have."
"We tried to find a dog that RESEMBLED our first one."

TO RESENT = to be upset or angry with someone or something that you think is unfair

"She RESENTS him for getting the promotion that she thought she deserved."
"Sometimes brothers and sisters RESENT each other for some small matter."
"He RESENTS co-workers because he thinks they are paid more than he is."

TO RESIDE = to live in a place

"I RESIDE in Columbus, but we also have a condo near Cleveland."
"I have cousins who RESIDE in Kentucky."
"Where does your family RESIDE?"

TO RESIGN = to quit a job or position in an official way

"Some of Donald Trump's staff were forced to RESIGN."
"He RESIGNED his job for health reasons."
"If you don't RESIGN, we will have to fire you."

TO RESPOND = to say or write something as an answer to a question, a letter, or so on

"What did you RESPOND when he asked you?"
"I sent an email to my cousin, but she hasn't RESPONDED yet."
"Do you want me to RESPOND to this letter?"

RESTLESS = not relaxed or calm; wanting change

"I had a RESTLESS night. I didn't sleep well."
"I'm getting RESTLESS in this house. Let's move somewhere else."
"If you kids are RESTLESS, you can go outside and play in the yard."

TO RESTRICT =1. to limit the amount of something

"The doctor told him to RESTRICT the salt that he uses."

2. to prevent someone doing something

"Parking here is RESTRICTED to employees only."

3. to allow someone to do only a particular thing

"You are RESTRICTED to playing in our yard. Do not go out of our yard."

TO REQUIRE -1. to need something

"We REQUIRE food, water, and shelter."

2. to be necessary for someone to do something

"We are REQUIRED to pay taxes."
"Students are REQUIRED to register for class."

TO REVISE = to make changes to correct or improve something

"I found some mistakes in your letter. Please REVISE it."
"The US needs to REVISE its tax laws."
"I REVISED it three times before I was satisfied."

TO ROAM = to wander freely with no particular place or destination in mind

"You cannot let your dog ROAM loose. It must be on a leash."
"We spent the afternoon ROAMING the city."
"Don't ROAM away from me. Stay nearby."

ROUGHLY =1. not gentle or careful

"He treats his wife ROUGHLY."

2. not exact, but close in number or quantity

"There were ROUGHLY fifty people at the party."

RURAL = relating to the country instead of the city

"I think I like RURAL areas more than the city."
"Her home is in a RURAL area."
"Most of Ohio is more RURAL than city."

TO RUSH = to do something quickly, to be in a hurry

"He had a heart attack, and they RUSHED him to the hospital."
"Look at the time! I have to RUSH!"
"People in the city all seem to be RUSHING somewhere."

S.

SCARCE = not plentiful

"Parts for his 1931 Ford are SCARCE."
"In hard times, money seems to be SCARCE."
"If trouble starts, let's make ourselves SCARCE!"

TO SCATTER = to separate and go different directions, or to place things in different areas

"The birds SCATTERED when I opened the door."
"He SCATTERED grass seed in his front yard."
"The people SCATTERED when the police arrived.

SCENIC = having a pleasing view of scenery such as mountains, lakes and so on

"His house has a SCENIC view of the Ohio River."
"The countryside is quite SCENIC around here."
"This part of the city is not very SCENIC."

SCRUMPTIOUS = 1. very delicious
2, of a person, very attractive

"She brought a SCRUMPTIOUS cake to the class."
"We had a SCRUMPTIOUS meal at the restaurant."
"That's a beautiful dress. You look SCRUMPTIOUS in it."

TO SEETHE = to be very angry while trying to control your anger

"She was SEETHING when she came out of the meeting."
"He began to SEETHE when he saw the scratches on his new car."
"Try counting to ten before you start to SEETHE."

SEGREGATION = the practice of keeping people of different races and religions separate from each other

"Before 1950, SEGREGATION was common in US schools."
"Many people fought to end SEGREGATION."
"Martin Luther King was a leader in the anti-SEGREGATION movement."

SELF-RESPECT = proper respect for yourself

"Always try to keep your SELF-RESPECT."
"He lost his job, but he didn't lose his SELF-RESPECT."
"How can you wear that? Where is your SELF-RESPECT?"

SETBACK = a problem that makes progress difficult

"He was getting well, but he had a SETBACK and had to stay home another week."
"The company has had some financial SETBACKS."
"It took several years to recover from their SETBACK."

SEVERE = very bad or serious

"We may have some SEVERE weather next week."
"She stayed home with a SEVERE headache."
"It was a SEVERE cut that required ten stitches."

TO SEW = to make or repair something with a needle and thread

"Can you SEW a button on my shirt?"
"He lost a finger, but the doctors were able to SEW it back on his hand."
"Some of the students are taking a SEWING class."

SHAKY =1. not strong or steady

"The baby took a few SHAKY steps and fell down."

2. weak and likely to break

"Be careful. That ladder looks SHAKY."

3. not impressive

"The team had a SHAKY start but is doing better now."

TO SHATTER = to break into many pieces

"He dropped the dish, and it SHATTERED on the floor."
"She felt that her heart was SHATTERED after her husband died."
"The dish SHATTERED on the floor. Be careful where you walk."

SHELTER = a structure that protects people or things

"We ran for SHELTER when it began to rain."
"They provide SHELTER for homeless people."
"He built a storm SHELTER in his back yard."

SHIFTY - having a not honest appearance

"That man has a SHIFTY look. Let's cross the street."
"My mother saw two SHIFTY men waiting for her to close the store. Later she learned it was her two brothers who didn't want to bother her."

TO SHIMMER = to shine with a light that seems to move slightly

"We could see the stars SHIMMER in the night sky."
"Her eyes were SHIMMERING in the candlelight."
"The sunlight SHIMMERED on the morning grass."

SHOT = 1. the sound of shooting a gun

"I heard a SHOT in the distance."

2. medicine received in a needle

"Did you get a flu SHOT this year?"

3. a try at something

"Give it a SHOT. Maybe you can do it."

4. a picture taken with a camera

"I got a SHOT of the children playing."

5. a small drink

"He drank a SHOT of whiskey and left."

6. in very bad condition

"These pants are SHOT. I need a new pair of pants."

SHOWCASE = a cabinet with a glass top and sides used in a store to display products

"Come see the watches in our SHOWCASE."
"They broke the SHOWCASE and stole the jewelry."
"The store owner keeps a gun hidden behind the SHOWCASE."

SIBLING = a brother or sister

"Do you have any SIBLINGS?"
"All my SIBLINGS are married."
"She's an only child. She has no SIBLINGS."

SIDEWAYS =1. with one side facing forward
"They took a picture of his face, then asked him to turn SIDEWAYS for another picture."

2. toward either the right or left side
"We had to turn SIDEWAYS to get through the crowd."

SIMPLE = not difficult, or plain
"It was a SIMPLE problem, easily fixed."
"The Amish people wear SIMPLE clothing, nothing fancy."
"The directions aren't SIMPLE. I can't understand them."

TO SIP = to drink slowly or a small amount
"The coffee was hot. I had to SIP it slowly."
"He took his medicine with a SIP of water."
"Give him a SIP, but not very much."

SITE =1. the place where something is, was, or will be
"The SITE of the new library is next to the school."

2. a place where something important happened
"This is the SITE where the treaty was signed."

3. a place used for a particular activity
"People are not allowed at the nuclear test SITE."

SKEPTICAL = having doubt about something
"Many people are SKEPTICAL of Donald Trump's ability."
"I'm SKEPTICAL about getting off work early today."
"He said he could do it, but I'm SKEPTICAL."

SKITTISH = nervous, easily frightened

"The cat was too SKITTISH to come out from under the car."
"I'm SKITTISH about putting my money in the stock market."
"He's a good horse. but something has made him SKITTISH today."

SLEAZY = not decent or respectable

"She's a dancer in a SLEAZY nightclub."
"This looks like a SLEAZY part of town. Let's keep going."
"She is dating a SLEAZY guy with no job and no money."

SLEW = In the Bible, Cain SLEW his brother Abel. But in its slang use, SLEW means a large number of people or things

"A SLEW of people were waiting in line."
"He had to buy a SLEW of books for college."
"There's a SLEW of cars in the parking lot. I wonder what is going on?"

TO SNUGGLE = to lie or sit closely together

"The boy SNUGGLED close to his mother."
"My wife and I like to SNUGGLE in bed before we go to sleep."
"Come sit beside me and SNUGGLE a little bit."

TO SOB = to cry and gasp for breath at the same time

"The little girl was SOBBING and couldn't stop."
"She always SOBS at sad movies."
"Please don't leave me," she SOBBED.

SOCIABLE = friendly; liking to be with and talking to people

"Be SOCIABLE at the party. Don't just stand alone."

"Everyone in our class is SOCIABLE."
"Our new neighbors aren't very SOCIABLE."

SOIL (noun) = the ground and dirt

"This is good SOIL for farming."

(verb) = to make dirty.

"He SOILED his clothes working on his car."

SOLEMN = very serious or formal in manner and expression

"The man's funeral was very SOLEMN."
"He was SOLEMN when he gave us the news."
"It was a SOLEMN ceremony to remember those who died in the fire."

TO SOLVE = to find the correct answer or explanation

"He SOLVED all the math problems."
"The police SOLVED the robbery and arrested three men."
"It's a mystery that has never been SOLVED."

SOURPUSS = a person who complains frequently and looks mad or unhappy

"Our neighbor is a SOURPUSS. Stay out of his yard and don't bother him."
"Quit being a SOURPUSS about it and cheer up!"
"The boss is a SOURPUSS today. I wonder what's bothering him?"

SPARSE = present only in small amounts

"People are SPARSE in some parts of the country!"
"Good restaurants are SPARSE on this side of town."
"Rain has been SPARSE this year. We may not have a good crop."

SPECTATOR = a person who watches an event, show, movie, game, and so on; a member of an audience

"SPECTATORS gathered to see the Pope's arrival."
"The SPECTATORS shouted when their team won the game."
"No, I'm not a player, I'm just a SPECTATOR."

TO SPECULATE = to think about something and make guesses about it

"Can you SPECULATE who might run in the next election?"
"We didn't see what happened; we can only SPECULATE."
"I hate to SPECULATE; give me some facts."

SPELL (verb) = to say or write the letters of a word or name

"Please SPELL your last name."

(noun) = secret words that are believed to have magical powers

"The witches cast a SPELL on the Queen."

(noun) = a period of time

"Come sit a SPELL. We'll have a cup of coffee and talk."

TO SPLURGE - to spend more money than usual on something

"I SPLURGED a little bit and bought a nice necklace for my wife."
"It's OK to SPLURGE sometimes, but not all the time."
"We can't afford to SPLURGE on a vacation this year. Maybe next year."

SPONTANEOUS = done or said suddenly without any thought or planning

"The necklace I bought was a SPONTANEOUS purchase."
"I'm not SPONTANEOUS most of the time, but only occasionally."
"It's better to have a list than to be a SPONTANEOUS shopper."

TO SQUABBLE = to argue about things that are not important

"The kids began to SQUABBLE about whose turn it was to go first."
"Do you ever SQUABBLE with your wife or husband?"
"I could hear the neighbors SQUABBLING through their open window."

TO SQUANDER = to use something in a foolish or wasteful way

"I SQUANDERED my whole afternoon playing on the computer."
"He SQUANDERED his paycheck buying drinks for his friends."
"Save some of your money and don't SQUANDER all of it."

SQUEAMISH = easily made to feel sick or disgusted

"Some people get SQUEAMISH at the sight of blood."
"My daughter is SQUEAMISH about spiders."
"My stomach is SQUEAMISH. I don't want to eat anything."

TO STAMMER = to speak with many pauses because of a speech problem or nervousness or fright

"She STAMMERED her name and ran out of the room."
"He STAMMERS when he is nervous."
"Calm down! You're STAMMERING!"

STANCE = 1. an opinion

"What's your STANCE on abortion in the US?"

2. the way in which someone stands

"She took a casual STANCE and answered all our questions."

STEAM (noun) = the hot gas that is created when water is boiled

"Be careful. The STEAM is hot."

(verb) = to cook vegetables or rice

"I STEAMED some vegetables for dinner."

(noun) = the strength or energy to continue doing something

"I've run out of STEAM. I need to rest for a few minutes."

AND TO BE STEAMED means to be angry.

"He's STEAMED because I forgot to buy his newspaper."

STRAIN (noun) = a feeling of stress and worry

"The hard work has been a STRAIN on her."

(verb) = to injure part of the body

"He STRAINED his back trying to lift the heavy box."

(verb) = to cause trouble or problems

"Losing their house has been a STRAIN on their marriage."

STRAND = a small piece of hair, thread, or so on

"Hold still. There's a STRAND of hair on your sweater."
"Don't pull on the STRAND. It's part of the sweater."
"I found a STRAND of hair in my food. The waiter took it away, brought me another plate, and they didn't charge me for my

meal."

STRUGGLE (verb) = to try very hard to do something that is difficult
"He fell in the river and STRUGGLED to keep his head above water."

(noun) = something that is difficult to do
"Sometimes it's a STRUGGLE to get up in the morning!"

STUBBORN = having or showing determination not to change one's opinion or attitude about something
"He knows he is wrong, but he's too STUBBORN to admit it!"
"My mother used to say that my father was a STUBBORN man."
"He's even too STUBBORN to come in out of the rain."

TO STUMBLE = to hit your foot on something that makes you fall or almost fall
"He STUMBLED on the loose carpet and almost fell."
"She STUMBLED on the stairs and twisted her ankle."
"He STUMBLED into the room and fell to the floor."

STUNNING = very shocking or surprising, or very beautiful
"Did you hear the STUNNING news about the accident?"
"She is a STUNNING woman."
"She wore a STUNNING dress."

TO STUTTER = to have a speech problem that causes you to repeat the beginning sounds of some words
"I c-c-c-c-can't hear you."
"There is a famous singer who STUTTERS when he speaks, but not when he sings."

TO SUFFICE = to be as much as needed

"This room will SUFFICE for our class."
"I didn't fix much for dinner. Will this SUFFICE?"
"This will more than SUFFICE. Thank you so very much!"

SUFFICIENT = to be enough

"Are there SUFFICIENT chairs for everyone?"
"You don't have to cook more food. This is SUFFICIENT."
"There wasn't SUFFICIENT time to do everything we wanted."

TO SUPPLEMENT = to add something to something to make it better or complete

"He took a second job to SUPPLEMENT his income."
"She takes vitamins to SUPPLEMENT her diet."

TO SURMISE = to suppose something is true without having evidence to confirm it

"I saw the open door and SURMISED that something was wrong."
"No one has called. Do you SURMISE that anyone will come to our party?"
"We SURMISE that he did it, but we're still looking for proof."

SURVIVOR = a person who continues to live after an accident, a war and so on

"The plane crashed into the mountain. There were no SURVIVORS."
"There was only one SURVIVOR of the accident."
"He's a SURVIVOR of two wars."

TO SWAP = to trade

"Would you SWAP seats with me?"
"He SWAPPED his watch for a necklace to give to his wife."
"That's not a fair SWAP."

TO SWELL (verb) = to grow larger

"The bee sting caused his arm to SWELL."

(adjective) = very good

"That was a SWELL party!" "Thanks for the SWELL dinner!"

TO SWINDLE = to cheat someone for money or property by telling lies

"He SWINDLES elderly people out of their money."
"Don't buy anything from him. He will try to SWINDLE you."
"The police are looking for the man who SWINDLED us."

TO SWELTER = to feel hot and uncomfortable

"We may be cold now, but we will probably SWELTER this summer!"
"Even the animals SWELTER when it's this hot."
"The workers were SWELTERING in the hot sun."

TO SWITCH = 1. to change from one thing to another

"I had to SWITCH doctors when I moved to Columbus."

2. to change from one thing to another by pushing a button or moving a lever

"I SWITCHED channels on the TV."
"I SWITCHED the car radio from my wife's classical music to hear some country music."

GRAMMAR BREAK: USING SHOULD, COULD, and WOULD
Officially, SHOULD, WOULD and COULD are the past tenses of shall, can, and will. They are used in other situations as indicated below.

We use SHOULD:
to express something that is possible
"They SHOULD be here next week."
"We SHOULD buy some extra food."

to ask questions
"SHOULD we call them?"
"SHOULD they be home by now?"

to show obligation
"We SHOULD drink 8 glasses of water every day."
"They SHOULD bring dinner when they come."

to make recommendations or give an opinion
"We SHOULD go to see your sister."
"The government SHOULD lower taxes."

We use COULD:

to suggest a possibility
"You COULD go with us."
"I COULD have left my keys in the car."

to ask questions
"Where COULD I have left my keys?"
"COULD you see the eclipse?"

to make polite requests
 "COULD you pass the salt, please?"
"COULD you open the window?"

We use WOULD:

to ask who, what, where, when, why, or how
"How WOULD you fix it?"
"What WOULD you do if you won the lottery?"
"Why WOULD you do that?"
"Where WOULD you like to go for dinner?"

to make polite requests
"I WOULD like a cup of coffee, please."
"WOULD you please sit down."

to ask questions
"WOULD you like more coffee?"
"WOULD you have dinner with us?"

in hypothetical situations
"If I had the money, I WOULD travel the world."
"I WOULD love a nice house in the country, away from the city."

to show intention or plan
"She said she WOULD be here at 9:00 AM."

t.

TABOO = not acceptable to talk about or do

"In many cultures, it is TABOO for a brother and sister to marry."
"Some companies make it TABOO for co-workers to date."
"At dinner tonight, let's make it TABOO to talk about sex, religion, and politics."

TADPOLE / POLLIWOG = a small creature that is born in and lives in water and grows up to be a frog

"We used to find TADPOLES in puddles of water."
"POLLIWOG is another name for a TADPOLE."

TAILLIGHT = one of the red lights on the rear of a car, truck, or other vehicle

"He drove away until all I could see were his TAILLIGHTS."
"She has a broken TAILLIGHT on her car."
"Can you replace a bad bulb in my TAILLIGHT?"

TENTATIVE = not definite; open to change

"I have TENTATIVE plans to visit my brother. I have to work out the details."
"It's still TENTATIVE, but we may be there next week."
"I made TENTATIVE reservations for 25 people. I have to call back if there will be more."

TO THREATEN =1. to say that you will hurt someone or do something unwanted if someone doesn't do what you want

"My neighbor THREATENED to call the police if our party gets too loud."
"The boss THREATENED to fire me if business doesn't get better."

2. used to say that something bad or harmful is likely to happen

"Those black clouds in the sky are THREATENING to rain."

TO TILT = to tip or move something so that one side is higher than the other side

"The picture on the wall is TILTED. Can you straighten it, please?"
"The dentist asked me to TILT my head back."
"Please don't TILT back in that chair. It might break."

TOMBOY = a girl who enjoys things that people think are more for boys

"When my daughter was growing up, she was a TOMBOY. She liked to play with cars and trucks and to climb trees."
"Were you a TOMBOY when you were a young girl?"
"My wife wanted a daughter who would wear fancy dresses and pretty shoes, but she got a TOMBOY!"

TOUPEE = a wig or a hairpiece worn by a man to cover a bald spot

"That man is wearing a bad TOUPEE."
"He bought a TOUPEE thinking it would make him look better."
"His wife didn't want him to buy a TOUPEE."

TRADITION = a custom of doing something that has been used by people in a country, a group, or family for a long time

"It is a TRADITION in my family for us all to get together on Thanksgiving Day."
"Some people make it a TRADITION to have a family reunion every year."
"What TRADITIONS do you have in your family?"

TRASH(noun) = waste or garbage
(verb) ="I had to TRASH my old pair of shoes."

"Put this in the TRASH, please."

In slang, TO TRASH someone means to say bad things or to criticize someone

"Many people are TRASHING Donald Trump."

TREASON = to try to overthrow your country's government or to help your country's enemies

"In the American Revolution, Benedict Arnold was an American General who quit the Army and went to fight for the British Army. That was TREASON."
"The soldier was executed for TREASON."

TRUCE = an agreement to stop fighting

"There has been an uneasy TRUCE between the two countries."
"She and her husband have been fighting. They need to make a TRUCE."
"They broke the TRUCE and started fighting again."

TRUSTWORTHY = able to be relied on

"Companies want to hire TRUSTWORTHY people."

"They thought he was TRUSTWORTHY, but he stole their money and left town."
"Dogs are known to be TRUSTWORTHY to their owners."

TURMOIL = a state of confusion or unrest

"There is a lot of TURMOIL in the Middle East."
"Her life is full of TURMOIL."
"The police tried to calm the TURMOIL after the shooting."

TYPICAL = normal, average, or usual

"I wore my TYPICAL white shirt every day ."
"It has been a TYPICAL day."
"It's TYPICAL of him to be here every day."

u.

UNEASY =1. worried or unhappy about something

"I'm UNEASY about the weather."
"There's an UNEASY situation between India and Pakistan."

2. not settled, or awkward and not relaxed

"There was an UNEASY silence when he entered the room."

TO UNDERTAKE = to begin or attempt something

"He would like to UNDERTAKE a world tour."
"That sounds like more than you should UNDERTAKE."
"She plans to UNDERTAKE a career in medicine."

URGE(verb) = to try to persuade someone to do something

"I URGE you to reconsider your plans."

(noun) = a strong need or desire to do something

"I have an URGE to visit my brother."

UTTER (adjective) = complete or total

"The day was an UTTER disaster." "The house was an UTTER loss."

(verb) = to say something

"He UTTERED something, but I couldn't understand him."

GRAMMAR BREAK: IRREGULAR VERBS
Most English verbs form the past tense by adding "-ed," "-d," or "-ied."

For example:

walk   walked
love   loved
marry   married

There are many verbs, which do not follow this pattern, and we call these IRREGULAR VERBS. There is no rule to follow for irregular verbs; you must learn them. Here are just a few:

VERB	PAST TENSE	PAST PARTICPAL
BE	WAS / WERE	BEEN
BECOME	BECAME	BECOME
BEGIN	BEGAN	BEGUN
BITE	BIT	BITTEN
BLEED	BLED	BLED
BREAK	BROKE	BROKEN
CATCH	CAUGHT	CAUGHT
CHOOSE	CHOSE	CHOSEN
COME	CAME	COME
DRAW	DREW	DRAWN
DO	DID	DONE
FALL	FELL	FALLEN
FEED	FED	FED
FIGHT	FOUGHT	FOUGHT
FIND	FOUND	FOUND
FLY	FLEW	FLOWN
FORGET	FORGOT	FORGOTTEN
FREEZE	FROZE	FROZEN
GIVE	GAVE	GIVEN
GROW	GREW	GROWN

HAVE	HAD	HAD
HEAR	HEARD	HEARD
HIDE	HID	HIDDEN
KEEP	KEPT	KEPT
LEAVE	LEFT	LEFT
LOSE	LOST	LOST
PAY	PAID	PAID
RIDE	RODE	RIDDEN
RING	RANG	RUNG
RISE	ROSE	RISEN
RUN	RAN	RUN
SAY	SAID	SAID
SEE	SAW	SEEN
SELL	SOLD	SOLD
SEND	SENT	SENT
SHAKE	SHOOK	SHAKEN
SING	SANG	SUNG
SINK	SANK	SUNK
SIT	SAT	SAT
TEACH	TAUGHT	TAUGHT

You can find lists of over 400 irregular verbs in books at the library or online on the computer.

I included the past participles because they are used with the auxiliary verbs is, was, were, have, and has. If you use one of these auxialiary verbs, you <u>cannot</u> use the regular present or past verb form, you must use a PARTICIPLE. The present participle is easy: it's the verb with "-ing" added [talking, driving, swimming. working]. The past participles are usually with "-d," "-ed," or "-ied," but many are <u>not</u> regular, and you must learn and use these as you learn to speak English.

Present Perfect tense uses HAVE or HAS with the past participle.
Past Perfect tense uses HAD with the past participle.
Future Perfect tense uses WILL HAVE with the past participle

V.

VAST = very great in size, distance, amount, or extent

"It's a VAST distance from Earth to Mars."
"She has a VAST knowledge about World History."
"The US National Debt is too VAST for me to imagine!"

VENTRILOQUIST = a person who seems to "throw" his or her voice so that his words seem to come from a large doll

"I saw a performance of a VENTRILOQUIST."
"If you watch TV and one of the "Got Talent" shows, you might see a VENTRILOQUIST from time to time."

VERSATILE = able to do many different things

"She is a VERSATILE actress who can play many different roles."
"He's a VERSATILE chef. He can prepare many different styles of meals."
"If I hire you, you must be VERSATILE and work with many different people."

VICE VERSA = a Latin phrase that means "the other way around."

"He doesn't trust his wife, and VICE VERSA." *[she also doesn't trust him]*
"Men can bring their wives, and VICE VERSA." *[women can also bring their husbands]*
"I don't like Robert, and VICE VERSA."*[Robert doesn't like me]*

VOLUNTEER (noun) = a person who does something without being forced or paid to do it

"I was a VOLUNTEER teacher at the language school in Dayton, Ohio."

(verb)= to offer to do something without being forced or paid

"She VOLUNTEERED to bring drinks to the party."

VOW (noun) = a serious promise to do something or to behave a certain way

"My wife and I exchanged marriage VOWS."

(verb) = to make a serious promise or to behave a certain way

"President Trump VOWED 'to make America great again.' "

W.

TO WADDLE = to walk with short steps while moving from side to side like a duck

"The goose WADDLED across the street."
"The man WADDLED out the door."
"When my wife was pregnant, she complained that she couldn't walk normally but could only WADDLE."

WAGES = the money paid to workers

"The men went on strike for higher WAGES."
"You can collect your WAGES on Friday."
"The government collects taxes on your WAGES."

TO WARN = to tell someone of possible damages or trouble

"He WARNED me not to do it."
"WARN me if you see a car coming toward us."
"The police WARNED the people to stand back."

TO WARP = to twist something into a different shape
SLANG = "He has a WARPED sense of humor."
= twisted; not normal

"If you leave a piece of wood outside, the sun and moisture will cause it to WARP."
"Use a water sealant on your outside deck to prevent the wood from WARPING."

TO WEAR = 1. to use or have something on your body

"He WEARS a white shirt to work."
"She is WEARING too much perfume."
"I WEAR a watch"
"I don't WEAR glasses."

2. to cause something to become thinner or weaker because of
   continued use

"The brakes on my car are beginning to WEAR. I will have to get new brakes soon."
"The carpet is badly WORN where we walk on it all the time."

WHILE = during the time

"Someone called for you WHILE you were out."
"WHILE I was showering, someone knocked on the door."
"Please don't call me WHILE I'm at work."

WHISKERS = 1. the hair that grows on a man's face

"He decided to let his WHISKERS grow."*[and his wife told him to shave!]*

2. the long hairs that grow near the mouth of some animals

"A cat has WHISKERS."

WIDESPREAD = common over a wide area or among many people

"Trade between countries has become WIDESPREAD."
"It's a WIDESPREAD belief that space travel will happen some day."
"The flu is WIDESPREAD across the US this year."

TO WILT =1. **to bend over because of not having enough water**

"Fresh flowers will begin to WILT after a few days."

2. to become weak and tired because of hot weather

"We began to WILT under the summer sun."

y.

TO YAWN = **to open your mouth wide while taking in breath, usually because you are tired or bored**

"The students in class all began to YAWN."
"I start YAWNING just before bedtime."
"Don't start YAWNING! You'll make me YAWN, too! YAWNING is contagious!"

YUMMY = delicious

"We had a YUMMY dessert."
"The food at the party was YUMMY."
"Dinner was just YUMMY! Thank you for inviting us!"

Z.

ZEALOUS = feeling or showing strong support for a person, a cause, or so on

"She is a ZEALOUS supporter of women's rights."
"He is ZEALOUS about his beliefs."
"The Ohio State football fans are certainly ZEALOUS!"

PART II:
IDIOMS, SLANG, EXPRESSIONS

a.

> **A LOT ON ONE'S PLATE** means to have lot to do, to be busy.

"I have a LOT ON MY PLATE this week. Can we reschedule our meeting to next week?"

> **A ROARING SUCCESS** means that something was very successful.

"The party was a ROARING SUCCESS! You should have been there!"

"Wouldn't it be nice if when this book is published. that it becomes A ROARING SUCCESS for me?"

> **ALL BARK AND NO BITE** means that someone's talk is more threatening than what he or she might actually do.

"Don't let him threaten you or make you feel bad. He's ALL BARK AND NO BITE."

> **AT THE CRACK OF DAWN** means very early in the morning.

"He always wants to leave AT THE CRACK OF DAWN. I don't know why we have to leave so early." A lot of men that I know like to do this. Ladies, is this a "man" thing? Do all men do this?

If we start on a long trip, I prefer to leave AT THE CRACK OF DAWN. I can't convince my wife that this is the best time! Guys, what about you?

b.

A BEEF. Yes, BEEF is the meat from a cow, but to have A BEEF with someone means to have a complaint.

"Hey, I have A BEEF with you! Your dog has been digging in my garden. Can you keep him out of my yard?"

TO BEAT AROUND THE BUSH means to talk around a subject without being specific.

"I hear you're thinking of moving" instead of "When are you moving?" Some people might say, "Quit BEATING AROUND THE BUSH and get to your point."

When I was dating my soon-to-be wife, I never did propose to her. I never asked, "Will you marry me?" Instead, I said to her, "If we keep getting along as well as we are, we should think about getting married. THAT was BEATING AROUND THE BUSH!!

TO HAVE BIGGER FISH TO FRY means to have more important things to do.

"I can't go shopping with you today. I HAVE BIGGER FISH TO FRY."

To be in one's BIRTHDAY SUIT means to be naked.

"She came to the door in nothing but her BIRTHDAY SUIT."

If you go swimming naked, we call that SKINNY DIPPING.

I was out in the country with a group of guys from college. We all went SKINNY DIPPING in the creek in our birthday suits!"

> **TO BREAK EVEN means neither to lose nor gain money.**

"I played poker with the guys last night. I'm lucky just to BREAK EVEN."

Many years ago, I worked with an old fellow who took me to the horse races and taught me a little bit about how to bet on the races. Sometimes I would win a few dollars, and sometimes I would lose. It was fun to try to BREAK EVEN!

> **TO BURY THE HATCHET means to make peace with someone and not fight any more.**

"He and his wife have been fighting, but I persuaded them TO BURY THE HATCHET and forget about fighting."

> **TO HAVE BUTTERFLIES IN THE STOMACH means to have a nervous feeling.**

"I have BUTTERFLIES IN MY STOMACH about talking to a large audience. Do you have any advice to calm me down?"

I didn't like to stand in front of a large crowd to talk to them. It always gave me BUTTERFLIES IN MY STOMACH. That all changed when we formed our family band, the Franz Family Fiddlers. We performed in front of many audiences. Our children played instruments and sang, my wife played guitar, and I played bass. I also became the announcer, and I learned to speak without butterflies! That has served me well since becoming an ESL teacher!

TO BUY or NOT BUY is a choice you make about a new car, but the slang BUY / NOT BUY means to believe or not believe.

"He gave me a story about why he was late, but I DIDN'T BUY IT."
"Yeah, I believed him; I BOUGHT his explanation."

C.

TO CALL IT A DAY means that a day's work has been finished and it's time to quit working.

"That's enough for today, guys. Let's CALL IT A DAY and come back tomorrow."

Similarly, TO CALL IT A NIGHT means to be finished for the evening or night.

"I was drinking with the guys, but I had TO CALL IT A NIGHT and go home."

TO CATCH SOMEONE'S EYE means to attract someone's attention.

"If I can CATCH the WAITER'S EYE, I'll have him bring you a cup of coffee."
"Her beautiful dress CAUGHT MY EYE."

CATCH YOU LATER! is a common slang "Goodbye" and promise to talk or see someone another time.

"Is Maria home?"
"No, she's at work"
"That's OK. I'll CATCH HER LATER."

If something is CATTY-CORNER, it is not directly across the street, but at an angle across the street, or on the opposite corner.

"The post office is CATTY-CORNER from the bank."

I like to use CATTY-CORNER when I describe the location of a place. My wife grew up in Michigan, and she likes to use KITTY-CORNER. I don't know if that's a Michigan thing, but either one is OK with me!

A CHANGE OF HEART means a change of one's opinion or a change in one's feelings about something or someone.

"They plan to get married, but recently she has had a CHANGE OF HEART."

TO CHEW ON in this sense does not mean to put in your mouth, but to think about something.

"He wants me to go into business with him, but I need to CHEW ON the idea before I decide"

CHOP CHOP means quickly, or hurry.

"Take this to the boss, CHOP CHOP."

English is known for borrowing a lot from other langusges. CHOP CHOP may have its roots in the Cantonese language from China, and it may be an English version of the Cantonese "chok chok." Once something gets in our language, sometimes it's difficult to know the actual origin.

TO CLAMP DOWN on someone or something means to put a stop or put an end to something.

"The new employee has been coming in late. Let's CLAMP DOWN on him before it becomes a problem."

TO CLIMB THE WALLS means to be extremely anxious or annoyed.

"The kids have been bothering me all day. I'm ready TO CLIMB THE WALLS!"

TO COOL ONE'S HEELS means to wait or to be kept waiting.

"My appointment was at 10:00, but I had to COOL MY HEELS until they called my name at 10:30."

I don't like COOL MY HEELS when I'm waiting for my wife or kids. I used to take my children to their music lessons, and I usually had to wait an hour for them to finish. I did that many, many times, and I never got used to it!

COPY THAT! is an expression that means "I heard you" or "I understand."

"I won't be here next week. Do you remember?"
"Yep! COPY THAT!"

A COUNTRY MILE means a very long way.

"My car ran out of gas, and I had to walk a COUNTRY MILE before I found a gas station."

d.

DEAD LAST means last place in a race or competition, usually far behind or long after the next to last.

"All the other runners finished by 5:00 PM, but I came in DEAD LAST at 10:00 PM."

DON'T GO THERE usually means not to visit a certain place, but we also use **DON'T GO THERE** to mean not to talk about something.

"I asked him about his divorce, but he said, "DON'T GO THERE." He didn't want to talk about it."

DOWN IN THE DUMPS means to be in a sad, gloomy, depressed mood.

"She's DOWN IN THE DUMPS because she lost her job. What can we do to make her feel better?"

TO DRAG ONE'S HEELS or TO DRAG ONE'S FEET means to move slowly or reluctantly because one does not want to do something.

"He's supposed to send thank you notes for his birthday gifts, but he's DRAGGING HIS HEELS. Let's clamp down on him and make sure he does it."

When I was growing up, my father had a gas station, and my brothers and I all had to work there, too. This was at the time when we would go out to the cars, pump the gas, wash the windshield, check the oil, and put air in the tires. I would sometimes DRAG MY HEELS about going to work at the station, but my mother would have none of that! She made sure that we always went!

TO DRAW A BLANK means to be unable to think of, or to remember something.

"I'm sorry, I'm DRAWING A BLANK. What's your name again?"

I went to my 50th high school reunion. It was hard to recognize many people. Some people say that women change the most, but I think men change a lot, too. It was a good thing we had name tags. Even though I knew them 50 years ago, I DREW A BLANK on a lot of people!

e.

An EAGER BEAVER is an enthusiastic person who works hard to accomplish something.

"The new employee is an EAGER BEAVER. I wish we had more workers like her!"

EASY ON THE EYES can be an attractive person. male or female. It can also be something pleasing to see.

"That painting is EASY ON THE EYES. It would be nice to see every morning when I wake up."

"That woman is very EASY ON THE EYES!" "Yes, she is. She's very beautiful."

> **TO HAVE EGG ON ONE'S FACE** means to be embarrassed by something one has done.

"I asked her and her mother to sit down, and she said, 'This is my sister.' "
"Oh boy, did I HAVE EGG ON MY FACE!"

> **EVERY NOW AND THEN** means sometimes or occasionally.

"EVERY NOW AND THEN we get together for lunch."

f.

> **TO FEEL BLUE or TO HAVE THE BLUES** means to be sad, unhappy, or depressed.

"I FEEL BLUE today. No one has come to visit me for a while."

> **TO FEEL LIKE A MILLION DOLLARS** means to feel well and healthy, mentally and physically.

"What a beautiful day! I FEEL LIKE A MILLION DOLLARS!"

> **FROM SCRATCH** means without the aid of something that is already prepared.
> "She didn't use a cake mix; she made the cake FROM SCRATCH." Similarly, **TO START FROM SCRATCH** means to start from the very beginning, to start from nothing.

"He lost his first business, but he's going to START FROM SCRATCH and try to open another store."

My mother always cooked FROM SCRATCH. She was a good cook, too, and she kept us all well fed. I've learned to cook a little bit, and I often try to make some of the things that my mother made!

g.

TO GET YOUR DUCKS IN A ROW means to get organized, prepared, and up to date.

"We have to GET OUR DUCKS IN A ROW before he will even talk to us."

This was a popular idiom to use when I was working in a government office. We often had to brief someone higher up in management, and we always had to have our DUCKS IN A ROW. If we didn't, the boss would angrily throw us out and tell us not to come back until we were ready.

TO GET IN THE LAST WORD means to say the final words in a discussion or argument, usually to end the matter.

"We talked for hours, but I GOT IN THE LAST WORD and settled our differences."

TO GET IT OFF YOUR CHEST means to talk to someone about a problem that has been bothering you, making you feel better.

"That has been bothering me for a long time. I'm glad to GET IT OFF MY CHEST."

GET ONE'S ACT TOGETHER means to get organized and prepared.

"He wasn't a good student in school, but he GOT HIS ACT TOGETHER and did very well at college."

TO GET UP ON THE WRONG SIDE OF THE BED means to get up in a bad mood.

"I don't know what is wrong with him today. Maybe he GOT UP ON THE WRONG SIDE OF THE BED."

GIVE IT A REST is a way to tell someone to stop talking about something.

"You've told me how you feel about it. Now GIVE IT A REST for a while."

TO GIVE SOMONE THE AXE means to fire someone from his or her job.

"They GAVE HIM THE AXE today. I hope he finds another job soon."

A GLASS CEILING is an unadmitted and illegal barrier to advancement, especially women and minorities.

"Barack Obama broke a Presidential GLASS CEILING when he became the first black man elected to the highest office."

TO GO FOR A SPIN means to go for a brief, leisurely drive (Usually in a car, but this expression also includes bicycles or motorcycles).

"It's a nice day. Why don't we GO FOR A SPIN this afternoon?"

Do people still GO FOR SPINS any more? Since the gas shortages and since gas is more expensive these days, I don't hear people talking much about this.

TO GO LIGHT ON or HEAVY ON is usually a request in a restaurant.

"Please GO LIGHT on the dressing on my salad, but GO HEAVY on the cheese."

If I say that my plans WENT SOUTH, I'm not saying they went that direction. If something GOES SOUTH, it means it turns bad or fails.

"Business at the new store WENT SOUTH, and they had to close."

GOODNESS GRACIOUS! is a mild exclamation of surprise, annoyance, alarm, or exasperation. (It's more polite than using coarser language.)

"GOODNESS GRACIOUS! Look at the time! I didn't know it was so late!"

A GUESSTIMATE is part guess and part estimate.

"My GUESSTIMATE is that he should be home by 6:00 PM."

A GUT FEELING is an instinct or intuition. a feeling or reaction, without a logical explanation.

"If you don't know the answer, use your GUT FEELING to pick the answer you think is best."

"I'm glad to see you! I had a GUT FEELING that you might be here."

h.

HANG IN THERE is an expression of encouragement to stay calm in a challenging situation.

I once gave a poster to our secretary that showed a kitten hanging on a limb with its paws, and the caption said, "HANG IN THERE, baby, Friday is coming!"

HANG ON can also be an expression of encouragement, but this is what we say when someone calls on the phone, and we go get something or someone.

"Yes, Charlie is here. HANG ON, and I'll go get him."

TO HANG ON EVERY WORD means to listen very closely and attentively to what someone is saying.

"She says she loves him, so she HANGS ON EVERY WORD he says. I hope she gets over that soon!"

HAPPY AS A LARK is a way to say that someone is very happy.

"He's HAPPY AS A LARK to have a car that he can use!"

TO HAVE A FEW usually means to have drinks alone or with friends.

"I stopped to HAVE A FEW after work. I'll be home soon."
"I remember times when I'd HAVE A FEW with the guys after work.

I'm glad I don't do that any more! I'll have a glass of wine with dinner from time to time, but not often. That's enough for me!"

TO HAVE A FLING usually means to have short sexual relationship with someone.

"The boss HAD A FLING with is secretary. His wife found out about it, and now she is divorcing him."

TO HAVE A GO AT means to try to do something.

"I see you're having trouble with that. Let me HAVE A GO AT it, and I'll see if I can fix it."

TO HAVE A HANDLE ON something means to have a clear understanding of it.

"Thanks, but I don't need your help. I HAVE A HANDLE ON it."

TO HAVE A LOOK-SEE is an expression that just means to look at something.

"How is the construction going? Let's ride over there and have a LOOK-SEE."

TO HAVE A SAY in something means to have the right to influence or make a decision about something.

"If I HAVE A SAY in it, I don't think it's a good idea."
"I don't HAVE A SAY in it. It's up to them to decide."

TO HAVE A SKELETON IN THE CLOSET means to have an embarrassing or shameful secret that you don't want to be known.

"You can ask me anything. I don't HAVE ANY SKELETONS in my closet."
"She found out that he has been married five times. That's the

SKELETON IN HIS CLOSET."

> **TO HAVE ONE'S WIRES CROSSED is to be confused or mistaken about something.**

"I thought my appointment was today, not tomorrow. I must HAVE MY WIRES CROSSED."

> **For two or more people TO HAVE THEIR WIRES CROSSED means to have a miscommunication resulting in a mistake of misunderstanding.**

"I think their fight is just because they GOT THEIR WIRES CROSSED."

> **TO HIT A BRICK WALL means to come up against an unsolvable problem.**

"Our project was going very well, but we HIT A BRICK WALL when we ran out of money."

> **TO HIT IT OFF with someone means quickly to become good friends.**

"I'm glad I introduced you to her. I knew the two of you would HIT IT OFF."

> **TO HIT THE GROUND RUNNING is to begin something energetically and with enthusiasm.**

"We need to hire someone who can HIT THE GROUND RUNNING. He or she won't need much training and can do a good job for us right away."

> **TO HIT THE ROOF means to be angry suddenly.**

"Your father will HIT THE ROOF when he sees what you have done."

HOLD DOWN THE FORT is an instruction for someone to take care of everything while the person in charge is gone for a short time.

"The boss told me to HOLD DOWN THE FORT while he goes home for a couple hours."

HOLD YOUR HORSES is a common idiom that means "stay" or "wait."

"HOLD YOUR HORSES! Before you go running out the door, make sure you have everything you need."

A HOT POTATO is a sensitive or controversial issue that is difficult to handle, and no one wants to deal with it, so it gets passed around from one person to another, like a potato that is too hot to hold.

"It's a difficult problem, so I'm going to pass this HOT POTATO to my assistant."

HOT UNDER THE COLLAR is another expression that means upset or angry.

"He's HOT UNDER THE COLLAR because he has to work this weekend. That upsets the plans he had."

HORNY is a somewhat impolite word meaning sexually aroused.

"He told her he was HORNY."
"She slapped his face and said, 'Not with me, you're not!' "

HOW ARE YOU DOING? HOW'S IT GOING? HOW'S EVERYTHING? are all common American greetings.

The easiest response to each of these questions is , "Everything is OK." You might also respond, "HOW'S IT WITH YOU?" All of this is said in passing without stopping to talk more.

If you hear a lot of HUBBUB, you're hearing the noise from a busy, active situation or a crowd of people.

You might walk up to someone in the crowd and ask, "What's all the HUBBUB?" Someone will try to tell you what is happening.

i.

I TAKE IT... is the introduction to a comment or question to ask for clarification of something.

"I TAKE IT that you are coming with us? I TAKE IT that Charlie won't be here today?" These are asking for confirmation: "Is this correct "

The IDIOT BOX is a name we give to the TV.

"He has been sitting in front of the IDIOT BOX all day."

IN ALL HONESTY is the preface to a stronger or harsher statement to follow.

"IN ALL HONESTY, I think you should break up with him and not see him again."

We use IN CASE to mean in order to be prepared for something else that might happen.

"Take an umbrella IN CASE it rains."
"Take my phone number IN CASE you need to call."

IN FINE FORM means doing very well.

Sometimes this is used sarcastically: if someone is drunk, I might say, "Oh, he's IN FINE FORM" when the opposite is really true.

He can't drive, he can't work, maybe he can't even walk... "Oh, he's in FINE FORM!"

If something happens IN THE BLINK OF AN EYE, it happens or is over very quickly.

"It all happened IN THE BLINK OF AN EYE."
"We had a fire at our house, and everything we owned was gone IN THE BLINK OF AN EYE."

To be IN THE DARK is to be not informed of something.

"The company doesn't tell us anything. They keep us IN THE DARK."

IN A FLUTTER is to be in a nervous or confused state.

"She's IN A FLUTTER because her family is coming to visit for the first time. She wants to be sure everything is just right."

IN THE DOGHOUSE is not a good place to be. Someone is angry with you!

"He forgot her birthday, and now he's IN THE DOGHOUSE. Maybe he'll have to sleep on the couch tonight!"

IN A JIFFY is in a short time.

"I'll be there IN A JIFFY!"
"Wash your hands. Dinner will be ready IN A JIFFY."

IN A SORRY STATE is to be in a poor, run-down, unfortunate condition.

"I went to see the house where I grew up. It was IN A SORRY STATE."
"My business is IN A SORRY STATE after I left my cousin to take care of it."

IN VAIN means without success or result.

"The doctors tried IN VAIN to save his life."
"All our work has been IN VAIN. They cancelled their order."

TO JUMP FOR JOY is to be very excited and happy.

"My son JUMPED FOR JOY when he saw his new bicycle."

k.

If you want to be informed or involved with something, ask others to KEEP YOU IN THE LOOP.

If you're working on a project and have been talking about it, you can let the others know that you want to stay involved or informed, you can say, "KEEP ME IN THE LOOP."

This is another idiom popular when I was working. The bosses always wanted to know what was going on, so we had to keep them IN THE LOOP.

KEEP IT UNDER YOUR HAT means to keep something secret and not tell anyone else about it.

"I heard that she's going to have a baby, but KEEP IT UNDER YOUR HAT. She hasn't told anyone yet."

KEEP YOUR SHIRT ON is a way to say stay calm, don't get excited. wait a minute, don't rush, or don't lose your temper.

"We'll be there in a few minutes. KEEP YOUR SHIRT ON."

To KNOCK ON WOOD is usually a physical action of rapping your knuckles on something made of wood, or sometimes just said as a wish for good luck. It's usually attached to another statement

"I hope she gets back safely, KNOCK ON WOOD."*[This expression has its roots in an ancient superstition that knocking on wood will keep evil spirits away]*

1.

THE LAST STRAW and THE STRAW THAT BROKE THE CAMEL'S BACK is the final difficulty in a series of difficulties, or the last problem that causes everything to collapse. *[imagine a camel being loaded down with much weight. Finally, one more straw will be too much and the camel's back will break.]*

"You have been late to work every day this month. Today is THE LAST STRAW! You're fired!"

To LEAVE IN A HUFF means that you are angry or upset and walk out of the room.

"She got upset with me and LEFT IN A HUFF. I'd better apologize and tell her I'm sorry."

TO LET SOMEONE DOWN means to disappoint someone.

"He promised to help me, but he didn't show up. He LET ME DOWN."

TO LET SOMEONE DOWN EASY is to give someone unpleasant or disappointing news while trying not to hurt his or her feelings.

"I know we have to fire her, but we have to think of a way to LET HER DOWN EASY."

LIKE TWO PEAS IN A POD means two people look alike or act alike.

"She and her sister are TWO PEAS IN A POD. They resemble each other, and they like to do the same things."

LISTEN UP! is a direction to pay attention and listen carefully to what I am saying.

"LISTEN UP, everyone! There will be no class tomorrow."

TO LOSE ONE'S MARBLES is to go crazy, to lose one's mind.

"I can't find anything anymore. Am I LOSING MY MARBLES?"

"He doesn't know what he is saying. I think he has LOST HIS MARBLES."

TO LOSE ONE'S SHIRT means to lose a lot or all of one's money.

"I played poker with my friends and LOST MY SHIRT."

"He LOST HIS SHIRT in real estate investments."

m.

TO MAKE A BEELINE FOR means to go straight to or directly towards something, just like a bee flies to its hive.

"He got to the restaurant and MADE A BEELINE to the bar to get a drink."

"As soon as we get home, I have to MAKE A BEELINE for the bathroom."

The slang use of MAKE IT is to attend something, or to be on time.

"Did you MAKE IT to the party?"
"No, I had to work. I didn't MAKE IT."
"I MADE IT home in 20 minutes."
"What time did you MAKE IT to work?"
"I got there at 9:00."

TO MAKE ONE'S DAY means to give someone great pleasure.

"Seeing you today MAKES MY DAY!"

"It MADE HER DAY to get the job!"

MY LIPS ARE SEALED. I won't tell anyone!

"I can't tell you what he said. MY LIPS ARE SEALED."

n.

NO DICE indicates a total refusal; no chance; certainly not.

"The boss said NO DICE to my suggestion."
"She asked for $20, and I said NO DICE."

TO NOT KNOW SQUAT about something means to know little or nothing.

"My wife DOESN'T KNOW SQUAT about changing a flat tire."

O.

OFF THE RECORD indicates that statements or comments are unofficial and not meant for publication. This applies to conversations as well. If I tell you something is OFF THE RECORD, I don't want you to repeat it.

"President Trump made his comments OFF THE RECORD, but the newspaper printed them anyway."

If a person is ON EDGE, he or she is anxious or tense.

"He's expecting an important phone call. He's ON EDGE waiting for it."

If something is ONE'S CALL, it's up to that person to make the decision.

"It's YOUR CALL whether we stay home or go out for dinner."
"If no one else decides, then it will be MY CALL. I say we stay home."

to be ON SOMEONE'S BACK means to nag or pressure someone continuously.

"The boss is ON MY BACK to get this finished today."
"My mother is always ON MY BACK to clean my room. Sometimes I get mad at her and say, 'GET OFF MY BACK!'"

ON THE DOT means at a certain time.

"I'll meet you at 2:00 PM ON THE DOT. I won't wait for you, so you'd better be ON THE DOT."

> For a machine or appliance to be ON THE FRITZ means that it is not working.

"Our washing machine is ON THE FRITZ. We have to call a repairman."

> Try not to be ON THE OUTS with anyone. It means to be not on friendly terms with them.

"Ana and Pedro had a fight, and now they are ON THE OUTS. I hope they settle things and will be friends again."

> Are we ON THE SAME PAGE? Do we agree?

"If you think that President Obama was a weak President, we are ON THE SAME PAGE. I think the same as you."

> If something is ON THE TIP OF MY TONGUE, I almost remember it, but not quite.

"I know we have met before. Your name is ON THE TIP OF MY TONGUE! Don't tell me! Is your name Elizabeth? I thought so! I knew I would remember!"

> OUT COLD can mean unconscious or sound asleep.

"He was OUT COLD for his surgery. He should be waking up soon."
"She's OUT COLD every night at 10:00 PM. Don't try to call her after that."

> Similarly, OUT LIKE A LIGHT means someone falls asleep very quickly.

"He's OUT LIKE A LIGHT. We won't hear from him until he wakes up tomorrow."

To be OUT OF STEAM or TO RUN OUT OF STEAM means to lose energy or interest to continue what you are doing.

"We've been shopping all day. I'm OUT OF STEAM. Let's go home."

The phrase OVER THE MOON means extremely pleased and happy.

"He called and asked her to go to the dance with him. She's OVER THE MOON!"

p.

PAR FOR THE COURSE means an average or normal amount, or just what one might expect.

"The mail is late again today."
"That's PAR FOR THE COURSE. The mail is usually late."

A PENNY FOR YOUR THOUGHTS is what we offer when we want to know what someone is thinking. Of course, this is just an expression. I've never seen money change hands!

"She was sipping her coffee and looking out the window. "A PENNY FOR YOUR THOUGHTS," I said to her.

"If someone says A PENNY FOR YOUR THOUGHTS to me, maybe I'll say, "Make it worth my while, and maybe I'll tell you!"

If something is very easy to do, we say it's A PIECE OF CAKE.

"Can you sew on a button for me?"
"Sure, no problem. It's A PIECE OF CAKE."

The slang use of PULL OFF means to accomplish or do something.

"The thieves PULLED OFF a bank robbery just after the bank opened."
"He graduated from college. I never thought he would PULL it OFF."

PUT A LID ON IT is a request to be quiet or to stop talking.

"Class, you are getting too loud. PUT A LID ON IT!"

r.

We've all encountered RED TAPE before. RED TAPE is the excessive regulations or rules usually associated with a government office.

"We have to deal with a lot of RED TAPE when we deal with the government."

TO RIDE SHOTGUN means to sit in the car in the front seat next to the driver. If several people, especially children, are starting to get in the car, one might say, "SHOTGUN," and that person gets to sit in the front seat while the others must sit in the back seat.

RIGHT UP ONE'S ALLEY means something is exactly like or is well suited to do.

"Teaching English is RIGHT UP MY ALLEY. I'm good at it, and I enjoy doing it."

A RIP-OFF is a bad deal. If someone **RIPS** you **OFF**, he or she cheats you by charging too much money for something, or by selling you something that is broken or damaged.

"I had to pay $200 for the concert. What a RIP-OFF!"

GRAMMAR BREAK: PHRASAL VERBS

> **PHRASAL VERBS**
>
> A phrasal verb is not just a single word, but two or more words together that function as a single verb. Phrasal verbs are quite common in English.

Here are just a few:
ACCORDING TO means as spoken by someone.
"ACCORDING TO Maria, we will have class on Friday next week."
"ACCORDING TO the newspaper, President Trump will be visiting our city."

TO BUNDLE UP can mean to wrap some things together, or to wear warm clothes.
"BUNDLE UP the newspapers and take them outside."
"It's cold outside. You'd better BUNDLE UP if you go out."

TO CHEER UP means to be happy.
"There's no reason to be sad. CHEER UP!"

TO COUNT ON means to depend on.
"I'm COUNTING ON you to come with me tomorrow."

TO BE DEVOID OF means not having something or completely without something.
"That man is completely DEVOID OF any honesty! Don't trust him!"

TO DOCTOR UP a recipe can be to add something to make it better.
"I DOCTORED UP the recipe with a little extra onion and garlic."

TO FEEL SOMEONE OUT means to try to learn someone's viewpoint or opinion.
"Try to FEEL HIM OUT about what he thinks of our idea."

TO GET BY means to have just enough of something so that you can do what you need to do.
"Her English isn't very good, but she GETS BY."
"I have just enough money to GET BY until my next paycheck."

TO HAPPEN BY means to pass, arrive, or come upon casually or by chance.
"I HAPPENED BY your sister in the grocery store."
"We were just HAPPENING BY your house and decided to stop and visit."

S.

TO SHOOT THE BREEZE and TO SHOOT THE BULL both mean to chat idly, to talk about unimportant things.
"Every now and then, it's fun to get together with my old friends and SHOOT THE BREEZE."
"When I was in college, I could always find someone who wanted to SHOOT THE BULL about one thing or another."

If someone has a SHORT FUSE, he or she gets angry quickly or easily.
"My father has a SHORT FUSE. Be careful what you do or what you say to him."

TO SIT TIGHT means to wait patiently (and not necessarily just sitting).
"SIT TIGHT while I get ready. I'll be just a minute. I'll be right back.

> **SCUTTLEBUTT is slang for rumor, gossip, or news.**

"What's the latest SCUTTLEBUTT? Is the company going to close, or move? What do you hear, or what do you know?"

> **If something is SECOND TO NONE, then it's the very best.**

"It's the best restaurant in town. It's SECOND TO NONE."

> **SO LONG! SEE YOU LATER! are both common "GOODBYES." We can also use both together at the same time. We can also say, SO LONG! SEE YOU TOMORROW or NEXT WEEK! or we can just say, SO LONG!"**

> **If something SELLS LIKE HOTCAKES, it sells very quickly or in large quantities.**

"The singer put out a new record that SOLD LIKE HOTCAKES on the very first day."

> **You can say that a subject is a SORE POINT with someone if the subject makes them angry or upset.**

"Don't ask him about his divorce. That's a SORE POINT with him, and he doesn't like to talk about it."

> **To SPILL THE BEANS means to tell a secret.**

"The party was supposed to be a surprise, but she knew about it. Who SPILLED THE BEANS?"

STICK AROUND means to stay or wait in a place.

"Can you STICK AROUND a few minutes after class? I want to talk to you."

If something STRIKES or HITS A NERVE, it makes someone feel a strong emotion such as anger, sadness, or so on when he or she hears or reads your comment.

"Your letter in the newspaper HIT SOMEONE'S NERVE. We've had lots of letters and phone calls in response to your letter."

t.

TA TA is another simple way to say goodbye.

"TA TA! SEE YOU TOMORROW!"

To TAKE A STAB at something means to give something a try.

"I'm having trouble fixing this. Would you TAKE A STAB at it?"

TAKE OFF is slang for leaving.

"It's getting late. I should TAKE OFF and get home before my wife gets worried."

You CAN TAKE IT TO THE BANK means that you can believe a certain statement or piece of information because it's definitely true according to the speaker.

"I heard from a good source that the company is closing. YOU CAN TAKE IT TO THE BANK."

To TAKE TO THE CLEANERS, like losing one's shirt, is an expression meaning to lose a lot or all of one's money.

"He put all his money in the stock market. The market fell, and he got TAKEN TO THE CLEANERS."

THAT'S ALL SHE WROTE is an expression used at the end of a job or project. This means that everything is over and there's no more to be said.

"That's it, guys. THAT'S ALL SHE WROTE. Let's go home."

TO THROW IN THE TOWEL is an expression that comes from the sport of boxing. The boxer's trainer throws a towel in the ring as a signal of defeat to stop the fight. We use the expression to say, "I QUIT. I'VE HAD ENOUGH. I CAN'T CONTINUE." A politician running for office sees that he is losing, that he can't win, so he says,

"OK. I'm THROWING IN THE TOWEL."

THE SHOE IS ON THE OTHER FOOT is used when one person is experiencing the same bad thing that he or she caused another person to experience.

"When the policeman was arrested, he knew what it was like to have the SHOE ON THE OTHER FOOT."

TICKED OFF is another of many expressions that mean angry or upset.

"He's TICKED OFF because his wife forgot to buy beer at the store."

TICKLED PINK, on the other hand, means delighted or very happy.

"I'm TICKLED PINK to see you!"

TO TIE THE KNOT means to get married.

"They've been together for a while. When are they going to TIE THE KNOT?"

u.

UNDER THE WEATHER means sick or not feeling well.

"I won't be in to work today. I'm feeling UNDER THE WEATHER. I hope I'll be in tomorrow."

UP TO NO GOOD means to be behaving in a dishonest or bad way.

"Those men standing in front of the bank look like they are UP TO NO GOOD. Should we call the police?"

w.

WAS MY FACE RED! is said by someone who is embarrassed about something.

"I forgot to wear my belt, and my pants slipped down in front of the class! WAS MY FACE RED!"

WASH YOUR MOUTH OUT WITH SOAP is usually a threat to children who repeat some bad language that they have heard. 'You shouldn't say words like that! I'm going to WASH YOUR MOUTH OUT WITH SOAP!" Of course, if an adult uses these bad words, you can say,

"You should WASH YOUR MOUTH OUT WITH SOAP!"

That's WATER UNDER THE BRIDGE means that whatever happened is past and forgotten, and it's not a problem or anything to be worried about now.

"Our argument last week is WATER UNDER THE BRIDGE. Let's forget about it and be friends again."

Who WEARS THE PANTS in your family? Who makes the decisions? Who is in charge?

"In my family, both my wife and I WEAR THE PANTS!"

If someone is WET BEHIND THE EARS, he or she lacks experience.

"He just graduated from school. He's still WET BEHIND THE EARS. We need to hire someone with experience."

TO WET YOUR WHISTLE means to drink something.

"I have coffee, tea, or juice. Which do you want to WET YOUR WHISTLE?"

A WHITE ELEPHANT SALE is often held by churches to raise money. This sale usually has a lot of odds and ends that people bring that don't fit or that they don't use any more. We like to say that one man's junk is another man's treasure! So maybe you'll find something you like at a WHITE ELEPHANT SALE, or maybe you won't!

WITHOUT A HITCH means without any problems.
"We made the trip and got here safely WITHOUT A HITCH."

WITHOUT A STITCH means naked, without any clothes.
"The little boy ran out of the house WITHOUT A STITCH!"

TO WORK OUT usually means to exercise at home or at the gym.
"I try to WORK OUT one hour every day."

We also use WORK OUT to mean OK or not OK.
"Everything will WORK OUT fine. Don't worry about it." "Things didn't WORK OUT between them, and they got a divorce."

y.

YOUR FLY IS OPEN is what you say to a man who has forgotten to zip his pants. If someone says that to me, I am embarrassed, but I turn around and zip my pants.

www.ingramcontent.com/pod-product-compliance
Lightning Source LLC
Chambersburg PA
CBHW070101080526
44586CB00013B/1153